Not All Bullies Yell and Throw Things

Endorsements

"If you leave work with a feeling of angst in your solar plexus, or you realize you have been holding your butt cheeks together all day, read Glory's book. You might find the source of the problem. You need to do the work you were hired to do, but you do not need to put up with bullying. These are two separate issues. Bullying is personal and does not belong in the workplace."

—*Dr. Jay Carter*
Author of the best-selling book, Nasty People
JayCarter.net

"Life is too short to put up with bullying behavior from someone at your workplace. Do something about it and start today. Buy this book, read it, and put its advice into practice!"

—*Kathy Noll*
Award-Winning Author of Taking the Bully by the Horns
KathyNoll.com

"I had a boss who required me to arrive before him (6 a.m.) and leave after him… every day. I asked if for three months I could get there on Fridays at 7:15, so I could help my wife by dropping our daughter off at school. 'You know the rule,' he said. 'We all have tough decisions to make in our careers.' Glory has wonderful storytelling ability. You'll shake your head, laugh, frown, & raise your eyebrows when you read about the challenges others have dealt with in the workplace—and discover ideas for handling your bully. By the way, before I made the decision to move on from that company, the CEO recognized the bully in our midst and fired that guy."

—*David Handler*
Success Handler, LLC

"I am glad to see someone writing about this subtle abuse at work. It often goes undetected so many times–it is not seen or caught, and therefore not believed. Glory's book is definitely worth the read."

—*Elizabeth Bennett*
Author of Peer Abuse Know More! Bullying from a Psychological Perspective
PeerAbuse.net

"Do you dread going to work every day due to the subtle bullying behavior of someone there? This book will give you practical steps to end the workplace bullying in your life."

—*Cynthia Starz*
Founder, Talent Starz Human Capital Consulting

Not All Bullies Yell and Throw Things

How to Survive a Subtle Workplace Bully

Glory Borgeson

PINNACLE
PUBLICATIONS, INC.

Pinnacle Publications, Inc.
P. O. Box 4224
Wheaton, IL 60189

Design: Wayne E. Johnson
wayneej@comcast.net

Editing: Thom Kudla
To a T Editorial Group
TTEditorialGroup.com

ISBN: 978-0-9820507-1-2

First printing 2015

Printed in the United States of America

10 9 8 7 6 5 4 3 2 1

Dedication

To Richard. The first person to teach me the difference between agreeing to disagree *agreeably* and agreeing to disagree *disagreeably*.

Don't be bluffed into silence by the threats of bullies. There's nothing they can do to your soul, your core being. Save your fear for God, who holds your entire life—body and soul—in his hands.

—Matthew 10:28, from *The Message*

Table of Contents

Acknowledgments

Several people have contributed to this book over a few years. (That's how long it took to write it.) From discussing ideas and concepts to actually helping me navigate workplace bullying, it's been a pleasure to get input and feedback from each person.

Without Ed Rogowski this book just wouldn't have come to life. Ed's leadership example, ability to put tough workplace situation into words, and willingness to come up with solutions that work well is uncanny. Reserved and funny at the same time, Ed helped to keep me sane through about 10 years of stories, of my own and from other people. He also reviewed this book extensively with a pen in hand more than once.

Thanks to Steve Ramel for a great review, executive level feedback, and always being a source of wonderful management ideas for the last 20 years. Spending time with Steve on the phone (and occasional lunches) helped me over several years to hone the difference between good vs. bad management practices.

Thanks to my editor, Thom Kudla, for the several edits, helpful feedback, and additional work (in the form of "to dos" for me) to make the book better and more helpful for readers, especially for targets. Thom also got me through a rough spot when I still had a disjointed book on my hands and wasn't sure how to proceed.

Thanks to my designer, Wayne Johnson, for creating another book project for me with painstaking details and great graphics.

To all of the people I interviewed who have been the targets of a subtle workplace bully: Thank you, thank you, thank you. I know you all want to remain anonymous so I won't mention your real names. You know I appreciate your taking the time to share your stories with me.

Of course, if it weren't for the workplace bullies in my life, this book never would have been written. I guess I should thank them, too. LOL!

Disclaimer

This book is designed to provide information about workplace bullying. It is sold with the understanding that the publisher and author are not engaged in rendering legal services. If legal assistance is required, the services of a competent professional should be sought.

The purpose of this book is to educate and inform. The author and Pinnacle Publications, Inc. shall have neither liability nor responsibility to any person or entity with respect to any loss or damage caused, or alleged to have been caused, directly or indirectly, by the information contained in this book.

All stories and anecdotes told in this book are either fictional or names and circumstances have been changed in order to make it impossible to identify the real actors. If you think you see yourself in this book, you don't.

1

You Might Not Even Realize You Work with a Bully

"Bullying...is abuse that is allowed to go on in our society because we do not take the steps necessary to solve it as a systemic problem."

—Jay Carter in *Nasty People*

After 15 years in a succession of jobs in the computer software industry, Beth liked her job. She couldn't say she had liked every job she had after college, but this current position she got two years ago was a good fit for her. The type of work, the amount of teamwork vs. independent work, some interaction with the companies' vendors, and managing a few employees had made the job a good choice and a good fit for her.

However, for the past few months, Beth had been experiencing some health-related symptoms that were unusual and seemed to have their roots in the workplace. For example, she was having difficulty sleeping, she became irritated easily with her employees and her family at home, she had a hard time concentrating on tasks at work (she is normally a good multi-tasker), she seemed to be losing some hair, and she also got sick more often than normal. Beth found that going to work was more stressful than ever before, and she felt that the symptoms were somehow connected to work.

When someone suggested one of her colleagues may be bullying her, she dismissed the notion. The reason she dismissed it was because she had read articles about workplace bullying. They described workplace bullying as including behaviors such as:

- Yelling at a person
- Using expletives when speaking to (or yelling at) someone
- Calling a person names
- Sexual harassment
- Threatening a person with bodily harm
- Threatening someone in other ways, such as threatening to destroy their career
- Using social media or email to demean someone

Since she wasn't experiencing any of those things, Beth concluded she wasn't being bullied by the colleague in question.

Then, why was Beth experiencing some of the common symptoms of being bullied?

It's time to define a new type of workplace bully—the *subtle bully* or "*bully-lite*," if you will. For a while, I referred to these people as "workplace jerks." But that title seemed too nice. They are bullies. Subtle bullies, but for all practical and stressful purposes, they are bullies.

You might have a subtle workplace bully at **your** *workplace.*

If you've heard and read about bullies in schools and businesses, the extreme ways in which their behavior is described may have led you to believe that the people causing you stress at your workplace are *not* bullies. It's possible your colleague doesn't yell at you, threaten you, berate you, or sexually harass you. Then why does your colleague cause you so much stress?

Are you in a situation similar to Beth's, where you are experiencing some of the stress symptoms of being bullied but have trouble pinpointing the source of the *bullying?*

The people who use the more subtle forms of workplace bullying are still bullies—and that is why you have similar stress levels, outcomes, and symptoms as people who have a full-on, obvious bully in their life. Your experiences are just as real and harmful to you as to any other target of a bully.

The longer you sit there and take it, the more stress they will cause you *and* the more likely they are to choose another person as their next target. You see, by not doing anything about it, you are actually enabling their behavior and rewarding them, in a sense. Why wouldn't they continue to target other people?

Aren't you sick and tired of being the target of a bully? It's high time you did something about it!

I want to address the *subtle bullies* and their targets. In this book you will learn how to identify a workplace bully and then develop and implement a plan to get out from under their devious ways and, hopefully, prevent these bullies from continuing their negative behavior.

I have experienced more than my fair share of *bully-lite* characters in the workplace. I first identified it and started researching and writing articles about it after about 20 years in the workforce. The more I studied workplace bullying and the more I identified and defined the actions of the *subtle bullies,* the more I realized I had experienced this type of character several times earlier in my career. I also realized I have been the target of a subtle bully a few times since starting my research.[1]

My experiences as a target of these characters led to the same familiar symptoms—loss of sleep, frequent headaches, loss of concentration, feeling anxious, and, one time, I even had chest pains while driving to work.

As I've spoken to many people about the topic of subtle workplace bullying, I've heard numerous stories from people who've been the targets of this type of bully; the stress they caused, the sicknesses, the job firings—it's awful!

I've also realized that subtle bullies exist not only in the workplace but also in neighborhoods, churches, synagogues, community centers, groups of friends, and families. While I'm specifically addressing *workplace bullies* in this book, you also can apply the principles to subtle bullies in other areas of your life.

For those of you with a subtle bully at work, I hope by reading this book you're able to put together a plan that goes way beyond just *coping* with a workplace bully. I want you to be able to figure out ways to get that person to stop bullying you and, if that is just not going to be possible, I want you to find a new job—either at the same company (away from the bully) or at a completely different company.

Exposure to a workplace bully, even in the short term and certainly in the long term, will undermine your confidence and your self-esteem. Their words and ways will wear you down both mentally and physically.

Consider what would happen if you were exposed to a low dose of carbon monoxide five days a week for many months. The toxin would get into your body and slowly break down your tissues and your immune system. It would eventually make you very ill and possibly cause you to die.

Subtle bullying at your job works in a similar manner. It slowly breaks down your confidence and self-esteem, making it much more difficult to do a good job. The stress it causes can lead to a weaker immune system and frequent illness.

The studies of stress caused by these subtle bullies have included reports of sleeplessness, irritability, headaches, weight loss, weight gain, hair loss, frequent illness, and more. In a report conducted by the Workplace Bullying Institute (WBI) in 2003, it showed that people who have been targeted by workplace bullies report their top five health problems as anxiety, loss of concentration, disrupted sleep, hypervigilance symptoms, and stress headaches.[2]

While most of these health problems are easily defined, hypervigilance might sound new or unusual. Symptoms of hypervigilance can include going over something many times, such as reviewing a report over and over, reading an email many times before sending it, or re-checking your work when one review should suffice.

A lot has been written about workplace bullies, those toxic types of people who yell, throw things, and harass others. But this more subtle type of bully—about whom most writers don't write and most researchers don't research—is difficult to define. These subtle types typically don't yell, throw things, threaten, or sexually harass others. But they do create a lot of stress for people who work with or for them. They adopt more passive-aggressive behaviors that might make it difficult to identify them in the workplace.

For those of you who work with bully-lite characters, one of the problems is spotting them. They can be subtle enough that their behavior goes unnoticed by coworkers, managers, and executives who have the authority to do something about it.

Many people in upper management get starry-eyed around high performing employees, such as top sales people and top sales managers. If these high-performing employees also bully their colleagues and direct reports, many executives turn a blind eye to the bullying behaviors because these employees get great results elsewhere. Upper management sees the bully's tangible results, such as higher sales, lower expenses, or on-time projects that are under budget, while overlooking the long-term costs to the company of keeping this person on the team. But despite their results, the manner in which they get those results causes long-term problems for the company. Their stellar results usually cost the company more in the long run.

The long-term problems can include a negative culture, excessive employee turnover, stress-related illnesses (and the healthcare issues that accompany it), poor engagement, and an inability to execute in a timely manner. If you don't engage regularly with upper management at your company, could it be that this type of subtle bullying behavior goes on at that level, too? Is bullying part of your company's culture? Does your company culture just care about results and not about people? Maybe your bully is simply mimicking the behavior of upper management.

The behavior of the subtle bully may be so subtle that it even is undetected by you! *You know there is something wrong, but what?* If it's hard to see/hear/sense the bully-lite behavior in the other person, then you can't challenge it. If you don't challenge or face it in some way, it will never stop.

Are you ready to get help with this stressful situation? Let's work together to put an end to subtle workplace bullying (or at least to minimize its detrimental effects on you).

Some Stories from Real Life

Here are a few stories that others have shared regarding their experiences with a workplace bully.

From Janet

Brett was not a good boss. I think he was not a good boss not because his sense of humor makes people laugh, but because his sense of humor involved making fun of people, which reminded me of my brother, Rob, and I was really used to that type of humor coming from a guy.

But the less I was around my brother (and especially after Rob got married and he seemed to slow down that type of humor), the more I realized that Brett's management style (and his use of humor) were not appropriate for a boss. But Brett got the laughs, so he continued doling out this type of humor.

Brett's sense of humor included clipping peoples' clothing with binder clips. He started with the small clips and moved up to progressively larger clips. It would have been funny if he would have only clipped his guy friends.

But he clipped his employees, including women. (This was the 1980s, when men wore business suits and ties to work and women wore business suits or dresses.) One time I saw him clip a customer's pant leg.

(Side note: I got a helium balloon at lunch one day at a restaurant where we went to celebrate someone's birthday. The balloon was already conveniently tied to a long string. I brought it back to the office, tied a small binder clip to the end of the string, and then gave it to someone to clip onto the back of Brett's shirt – you know that little piece of fabric on the back of a man's oxford shirt? Clipped it right on. He kept thinking he felt something on the back of his neck, but whenever he touched his shoulder or neck, nothing was there. He'd look to his left and his right, but couldn't see anything. *Was it a bug? A piece of lint?* I kept a straight face as he spoke to me with that balloon floating above his head. It was payback, baby!)

Brett made funny comments about people in front of others at meetings or out in the open around cubicles. These were often funny pot-shots. They were rarely aimed at the guys he considered to be his friends. The pot shots were mostly aimed at the men who reported to him but were not his friends and also at some women. (Sometimes the funny pot-shots were aimed at men or women who did not report to him, but were intended to turn people who reported to him against the target.) The problem was that he really *was* funny.

Brett did other things to me to tarnish my reputation at the company. It was awful.

I found myself getting a bit anxious to go to work and even to get up in the morning Monday through Friday. (I didn't feel anxious when Brett had a vacation day.) By the time I decided to look for a new job outside the company, I was even feeling a little depressed and having headaches too often.

It took me a long time to find a new job to get out of there. When I finally quit, I cried from relief when I got home.

I've worked with some really funny people but most of them didn't make fun of others (or if they did, they only did it to their work friends and it was a mutual ribbing). Do you have a boss who is funny but uses his sense of humor in a bad way on you? Does he try to get other people on his side against you by being funny and getting others to laugh with him?

From Andrea

Tina took her frustrations out on other people, often acting cold or mad (and we wouldn't know why). Later, after finding out what she was mad about, I realized that she had good reason to be mad, but she directed her madness at the wrong people.

Tina let one of my co-workers complain to her about me. Tina told me about it and then refused to tell me who the person was. I told her I did not agree with this at all. (The person complained that I wasn't being friendly enough in the office.) Besides the fact that we traveled a lot, I thought I spent plenty of time talking with people and "shooting the breeze." I also told Tina that I came to the workplace to work—not to make friends, and that if I *happened* to make friends with anyone, that was a bonus. But it was not the primary purpose for which I was there. I said again that I was not happy this person did not come to me first, but went to Tina to talk about me. I wasn't happy that Tina listened to this person rather than stopping her and telling her to discuss it with me first and I wasn't happy that Tina would not tell me who the person was. That was how the conversation ended.

A few days later, Tina brought it up again, stating she had thought about it more and decided that the other person had a "college-like" state of mind (read: *immature*) and was wrong in her thinking. So basically, Tina dropped it after re-thinking it.

Fast-forward about 9 months later. Normally we

trained a group of people on software and then supported the same group when they went "live" on the software. But I was told to support a group of people I hadn't trained and who hadn't been trained well.

It was a mess getting the employees in a group I hadn't personally trained to use the software they didn't understand. In the middle of this mess, Tina was not supportive, and instead made a comment to me (in front of three other people) referring to "that time" when someone else felt I wasn't being friendly. (What?!) This was months after she verbally recognized that the person who made the "college-like" statements was being immature and she dismissed that co-worker's comments. Now she fished it out of the garbage again.

When I told this story to a close friend of mine (who was also a counselor), he commented that Tina' actions were dysfunctional. She drudged up something old that she had buried (and which she should not have contemplated in the first place).

With the lack of support from my boss, I wasn't sleeping well. I knew that a colleague had Tina's attention to tell stories to get Tina to be against me, but I didn't know who was saying these things. I found myself second-guessing who was going behind my back and feeling somewhat nervous when around the person I suspected.

I found myself avoiding Tina as much as possible.

Do you have a boss who allows coworkers to tell her untrue stories about you? Does that boss put an end to these tall tales? Or does she not even try to find out the truth?

Like a dysfunctional family member who feeds off of secrets and ganging up on you, you can't win with this type of person as a boss. This workplace bully will look for people to feed her information against you in order to have an alliance, of which you are not a part.

Does someone at work do this to you?

———————

From Kathy

A company I worked for hired very immature administrative assistants. One sales manager told me much later that they liked the pretty younger women and hired them so that they could "look" at them all day and flirt with them. These admins treated most of the women in post-sales and pre-sales consulting very differently from the men. (There were only five of us and we traveled.) The admins would help the men by getting them their office supplies (I had to practically beg to find out where the supplies were stored), made sure the men's expense reports were entered timely (mine were processed late two months in a row, and I finally had to go to the general manager to get money to pay my credit card bills on time), and generally gave the men more support than the women. (Were we women invisible)?

One time a female colleague came over to me and said, "Come here a minute. I want to show you something." I followed her to a newly hired male employee's cubicle where a large pile of office supplies was left on his desk by an admin. Nice. Meanwhile I had to beg for Post-It® notes.

Knowing that the male bosses liked these young admins, I figured that telling the bosses about my experiences could backfire. I felt mostly alone there. My indirect way of alerting the bosses were to, for example, ask for an advance in order to pay the travel expenses on my credit card bill which were due before I was reimbursed because the admin didn't process my expense report on time (though she had it in time) and to make a point of requesting supplies. I think the subtleties were lost on the bosses but I did think, at the time, that pointing out the admins' actual behaviors could be risky for me.

Even though there were four other women at my level, we traveled often so I didn't work with them every day. I didn't have any real administrative support that I could count on. In a sense the admins were mini-bullies. I experienced a low dose of lethargy while at this company due to this lack of support and what often felt like the admins treating a few of us this way on purpose.

Before this experience I thought bullies at work would be bosses who bullied their employees. But I learned that even administrative assistants can choose a few targets to bully.

Is your workplace bully not actually your boss but someone who is in a support role and works behind your back to undermine you? By the time you figure out that this bully is up to something bad, she might have already ruined things for you. Whether you can make the situation change depends on in whose eyes the final opinion of you rests and how seriously that person takes the messages and opinions of this subtle bully.

From Anita

I took a job at a government agency that was in the field for which I received my bachelor's degree. This was a great job at a large organization and I was excited to be in a position for which I had been trained.

Unbeknownst to me, one of the candidates for the job was a mutual friend of two of my colleagues. They were very upset that I got the job instead of their friend. Their bad feelings about my hiring led to their terrible treatment of me. They put down my work and me as a person. This continued daily for weeks. I didn't know what to do so I didn't do anything, such as talk to my boss about it or anyone else at work. I was young. My friends didn't know how to advise me.

While I used to only drink on the weekends, I began having a drink or two every night. Then I started going out at lunch and drinking on my lunch hour. At night I didn't sleep well. I was really getting depressed. Finally, I quit without even having a new job.

I never got another job in my field.

When Glory told me she was writing this book, 10 years had passed since I quit that job. But just thinking about it and telling the story, I got tears in my eyes. I now realize that, while I still had that job, there were two people in the larger organization I could have contacted about finding another position and transferring. But I was in so much distress at the time that I wasn't thinking straight. I told Glory I needed a book like she was writing (and I needed it when I was going through it) in order to help me separate my feelings from the situation so that I could deal with the real issues and make a better decision regarding how to proceed.

I think with better ideas and guidance I could have figured out ways to cope while I planned how to change jobs within the organization. Then I would have saved my career.

Is your bully a colleague? Does he say things to get you down? Does he do things to damage your work or your reputation? Maybe you're finding that you're choosing to cope by adopting unhealthy habits. This is a bullying situation gone awry.

From Mike, posthumously

(This story was told to me by a former colleague of Mike.)

An operations director at a large corporation was known by many people at the company to be a bit high-strung. She erroneously believed her employees were trying to mess up her career at the company, which led her to be an ineffective leader and boss. Most people just tolerated her.

One employee felt stressed by this director's behavior and also felt as if he was her target. The director didn't yell or call anyone names. She had negative ways of expressing her displeasure, however, and didn't work toward solutions very well with people with whom she had conflict. This particular employee experienced so much stress from working for her that he was diagnosed with a disease that is known to have origins in high levels of stress. After a short time, he died. His family specifically requested that his boss not be present at the wake or funeral.

Death-by-workplace-bully. Terrible. This is the ultimate in stress caused by a workplace bully that leads to a stress-induced illness which leads to death. While most bullying targets won't suffer to this extreme, there are plenty of instances of connections that start with workplace bullying that ultimately leads to the target's death.

———————

These stories from real life may have stirred memories and emotions of your past or current experiences of being bullied at work. Bullies will derail your career, harm your health, and make your life miserable.

It's important for you to learn to manage a workplace bully or to get away from them entirely for your own health, career, and well-being.

Behaviors of a Subtle Bully

If you wonder if someone you work with now, or worked with in the past, is a subtle bully, let me ask you something: Have you ever heard the potential bully saying or doing any of the following?

- Making employees feel fear
- Lying or embellishing the facts
- Making fun of other people
- Creating a "frat-house" environment (Note: a frat house environment can include practical jokes, casual work rules applied to "frat" members, an emphasis on partying, exclusionary practices, joking at others' expense, or other unprofessional behavior.)
- Claiming people don't like working with you, when actually it's only him or her and possibly one other person who don't like working with you
- Not being supportive
- Not willing to roll up their shirtsleeves to help or give helpful ideas or advice
- Micro-managing—involves themselves in minutiae
- Projecting their dysfunctional understanding of work-place relationships onto others
- Demands to know details (and even approve them) that other bosses at their level wouldn't dream of being involved in
- A high-level person, such as a vice-president, who tweaks your Excel spreadsheets (e.g. adjusting column widths) and gets involved in other small tasks that don't belong to him
- Blames others for poor communication, but any lack of communication is his fault and sheds light on his extreme need to control small details
- Never or rarely accepts your ideas. Your ideas are either treated as non-existent or are put down.
- Lack of vision and/or the ability to think strategically so she instead focuses on tactical issues at a micro level because it's the only thing she can control
- Rather than just give advice to a lower-level employee who asks for advice and wants him to be a sounding

board, he gets involved (think: third wheel), writing lengthy emails on behalf of the employee
- Creates an environment of secrecy that leads to fear which then leads to mistrust
- Creates an "us vs. them" mentality to get people on their side and against their targets
- Takes credit for your ideas
- Isn't willing to allow you access to senior management without them being present or giving their prior approval

This list of subtle workplace bully behaviors is not exhaustive. It's an example of the types of things someone might be saying or doing that is leading you to experience the symptoms of being bullied.

Were you able to identify behaviors of your workplace bully from the list above? We'll examine a more detailed list of subtle workplace bullying behaviors in the next chapter.

What is the Bully's Process for Breaking a Target Down?

Kim scheduled a meeting of seven people that included her boss, Don. She would be leading the meeting using a projected slide deck and scoping out some data on a white board. While leading the meeting, Don interrupted her, stood up, and took a marker to the white board. His posture, demeanor, and words were more intense than a person who was simply participating in the meeting. He actually took over the leadership.

Later that day, Kim asked to have 15 minutes to speak to Don. She made it clear that she was leading the meeting and when he chose to take over the leadership, he undermined her in the eyes of the others who were present. He interrupted Kim to say she wasn't getting to the important part of the data and that was why he interjected. Kim clarified the difference, in her mind, between participating in the meeting and taking over the leadership of the meeting, again reiterating what the takeover did to her. She requested that he not do that again. He agreed.

(She didn't know how it would turn out in the future, but she felt certain that if she didn't say anything now, he would continue to walk over her again.)

Meanwhile, Alice had a similar experience with Don. The idea of talking with him about what happened, how she felt about it, and what she would prefer for him to do in the future made her feel sick to her stomach. The idea of just not talking about it with him at all stopped her stomach from feeling badly, but her anxiety level remained elevated.

Don continued to do little things to Alice that undermined her authority in others' eyes, put down her abilities just a little bit, and worked to lower her confidence in herself and in her work. He disagreed with her often in meetings, didn't acknowledge when she raised a good point or issue, replied to group emails with responses that didn't support her initiatives, and took too long to respond to her requests.

A workplace bully first looks to identify people who will make a good target. They find people who don't confront others, don't assert themselves, and will just take the bullying behavior.

Next, the workplace bully will throw out a zinger or two or three—they'll try a few choice behaviors that could be considered subtle bullying to see what the potential target does with it. If the person just takes the zinger from the workplace bully, then the workplace bully has established that the individual is a good target.

Some subtle bullies are fully conscious of what they're doing. These people bully others as if it's a game.

Other subtle bullies don't actually realize they're targeting someone with bullying behavior. Once they've unconsciously chosen to subtly bully someone, however, they continually choose new targets. Bullying other people becomes a regular behavior pattern they're not fully aware of.

Both the fully conscious and unconscious workplace bullies choose targets, whether they realize they're choosing a target or not, who will take the bullying without pushing back. Once they have a target for whom two or three bullying actions stick, they repeat the behaviors, especially the tactics that have worked on targets in the past to break them down.

Who is Likely to Become the Target of a Bully?

Psychologists, psychiatrists, and counselors who've worked with the targets of workplace bullies realize that targets come from a wide variety of backgrounds in terms of prior experiences with bullying. Some targets have never been bullied before their first experience with it as an adult in a workplace setting. Some were bullied some time in their school experience, but not by a family member. And others were bullied by someone in their family, usually by a parent.

Studies by Ruth and Gary Namie from the Workplace Bullying Institute (WBI) found that one-third of the targets of workplace bullies reported they have never been bullied by anyone before the current bullying situation at their job. Of the rest, they had experienced some form of bullying prior to the workplace; 44% were bullied by either a parent or sibling, 19% were bullied by a schoolmate or teacher, and the last 4% were bullied by a babysitter, neighbor, or someone else.[3]

People who experienced some type of bullying in childhood are more likely to tolerate bad behavior from others in adulthood, whether by a spouse, a colleague at work, or by a "frenemy" (that's a really bad friend!).

Additional studies by the WBI found that while a person is growing up, if their personal perspectives are disregarded by important people in their life, similar behavior and verbal taunts from a workplace bully later will most likely be tolerated rather than confronted.

If you've never been bullied before and your first experience being bullied is by an adult in the workplace, you still need to consider whether you're the type of person who will stand up to the bully's behavior or if you will back down. If you have experienced bullying during your childhood or teen years, it's high time you made some changes (scary as those changes might be).

BullyOnline.org has sought to overturn myths about bullies and targets. Their work has revealed that targets of bullies are strong, independent people who go to work in order to work, not to play politics. Targets assume all of the people they're working with at their jobs are rational human beings with whom they can have conversations to settle disagreements. Targets are not overly sensitive. Rather, lengthy exposure to bullying behavior leads to such increased stress that makes it difficult for the target to successfully negotiate with the bully.

Anybody can become the target of a bully. Bullies look for people who won't stand up for themselves or who will only stand up for themselves once and then stop. Bullies thrive on their role being successful which only works when someone doesn't stand up to them.

The Proof is in the Data:
Bullies are Hazardous to Your Health

Before we go any further, let's look at a few more statistics that will help you realize you're not alone in your experiences with a bully and will validate what you've been going through.

Earlier, you read the top five health issues reported by the targets of bullies in a 2003 study by WBI. In 2012, they surveyed 516 targets, also asking if they were treated by a physician or a licensed mental health professional for their work-related symptoms. Of those, 71% saw a physician and 63% saw a mental health professional. In this survey, their top 15 symptoms were:

- Anticipation of the next negative event
- Overwhelming anxiety
- Sleep disruption
- Loss of concentration or memory
- Uncontrollable mood swings
- States of agitation or anger
- Pervasive sadness
- Heart palpitations
- Insomnia
- High blood pressure
- Obsession over personal circumstances
- Intrusive thoughts in the form of flashbacks or nightmares
- Loss of affect (flat emotional responses)
- Depression
- Migraine headaches

Symptom clusters were also reported by one-half or more of the study group as:
- Post-traumatic stress disorder symptoms
- Clinical depression
- Anxiety
- Cardiological problems
- Loss of loyalty

Symptom clusters reported by less than one-half of the study group included:
- Violence toward self or others (or thoughts of such)
- Self destructive behaviors

Many reported diseases and conditions worsened by the stress of the bullying such as auto-immune disorders (i.e. fibromyalgia, IBS, Crohn's, multiple sclerosis), diabetes, eating disorders, and a variety of types of headaches.[4]

Do you identify with any of these things?

Several pages ago you read some stories about other people who've been the target of a subtle workplace bully, including the symptoms they experienced as a result. In thinking about the symptoms of being bullied, please reflect on the months you've been in contact with your bully and whether the symptoms listed sound familiar to you.

Thinking through my own history with subtle workplace bullies and looking through the list of symptoms, I know I've experienced anticipation of the next negative event, anxiety, sleep disruption, loss of concentration, feeling agitated, chest pain, insomnia, and migraine headaches. The chest pain symptom surprised me because my heart scans have always been clear. I felt the pressure while driving to work one morning. Because I was in the middle of writing this book, I immediately knew why I had the symptom.

Any combination of these symptoms leads to lower resistance to disease and a higher rate of aging. This is one of the reasons why the bullying has to stop: It is bad for your health and well-being.

Pay Attention to Your Stress Signals

What are the stress signals or symptoms you've experienced? It's important to identify your stress responses and then:

- Don't try to tough it out
- Don't ignore stress signals
- Don't think the stressors are temporary and will
  go away without being addressed

Just like a pain in your shoulder is a warning that something might be wrong in your shoulder (and you should have it checked out by a medical professional), so, too, are all of these warning signals of stress that tell you your health will be in danger if you don't find a way to end the bullying.

If a doctor determines you are getting ill because of work-related stress, don't file a workers' compensation claim. Your company's human resources department might push you to do so but in many states in the U.S., if you file for workers' compensation you won't be able to file a lawsuit later (if it comes to that). Contact an employment attorney for advice.

Now That You See You're Being Bullied, Use this Book to Arm Yourself

Awareness that you're being bullied at work, even in subtle ways, is an important first step in putting an end to it.

The information in this book is a set of tools to help you deal effectively with a workplace bullying situation. By reading this book and working through the ideas presented, you will:

- Learn to identify behaviors in someone at your workplace who might be a subtle workplace bully.
- Confirm you are *not* crazy. Rather, someone is bringing you down and might be doing it in subtle ways.
- Gain tools and action items to stop the workplace bullying in your life.
- Receive encouragement to take the steps you need to take to bring positive change to your career and daily work life.

While I cannot make promises or guarantees that your situation will change for the better, I am hopeful!

When you read a book like this, you will be doing some *self-coaching*. To get a framework around that, I'll fill you in on what coaching should do for you (when it's done well).

Coaching has four outcomes: *Awareness, Purpose, Competence,* and *Well-being.*

A workplace bully will aim to systematically destroy these four areas of your life.

Awareness: This is awareness of both yourself and of the environment and people around you. Awareness gives you the ability to correctly assess and interpret what is going on inside of you and around you.

Purpose: By having a solid sense of purpose you will know deep inside that what you are doing in your work has meaning and that you're a valued contributor.

Competence: Knowing you are highly competent in your work is an important outcome of coaching—to be able to perform your job well and to know that you are competent in your field.

Well-being: An overall sense of well-being in your work is the fourth outcome of good coaching. Your work and profession should provide you with a sense of well-being every day.

Do you see how all four of these outcomes of coaching are important if you are to have a successful career, waking up every day and looking forward to working in your profession with the people who are part of it? And do you see how workplace bullies aim to stop you from attaining any of these outcomes?

———————

Next, let's have a little more fun at the workplace bully's expense! I'm talking about revealing who they are and not letting them hide behind their façade.

2

What is a "Subtle Workplace Bully"?

"...although some assholes do their damage through open rage and arrogance, it isn't always that way. People who loudly insult and belittle their underlings and rivals are easier to catch and discipline. Two-faced backstabbers like my colleague, those who have enough skill and emotional control to save their dirty work for moments when they can't get caught, are tougher to stop—even though they may do as much damage as a raging maniac."

—Robert I. Sutton in *The No Asshole Rule*

Recognizing a workplace bully is the first step you need to take before deciding what you want to do about it. Varying levels of difficult managers exist in the workplace. When you picked up this book or saw it online, looked at the front and back covers, or perused the table of contents, perhaps you remembered bosses from your past who fit a particular description. Or maybe you thought about a manager who seemed worse.

A Subtle Bully is Still a Bully

The Internet is overflowing with stories about bosses who are called "toxic." The toxic boss is an aggressive bully. His behavior is obvious to most people. He yells, makes inappropriate comments to people, and offends many. There is nothing passive about this type of person. A toxic boss is an *obvious* bully. He may exhibit outrageous behavior. Occasionally, people who report to him may not feel safe.

One of the best examples of a toxic boss comes from Azita Zendel, who at one time worked as an assistant for Oliver Stone. In her book, "How to Survive the Toxic Boss Syndrome," Zendel teaches readers "how to manage compromising workplace situations involving sex and drugs, what to do when your boss' best friend pulls down his pants in your office, and what to say to your boss if he asks you to take a bag through Customs of a small international airport into which you've just flown."

Did I say toxic bosses are outrageous?

Another example of a toxic boss is the late Steve Jobs of Apple, who was often described as "yelling, ranting, and berating people," and giving out blistering verbal attacks loudly and clearly.

A former Apple employee, Erin Caton, wrote on her blog, "I.M.H.O," a story saying that Steve Jobs, who she didn't recognize at the time, cut in front of her in the cafeteria line. She turned to her coworker and said, "Who is this douche?" Her coworker whispered, "That's *Steve*." Another time, while yelling at her team that had a poor product launch, he said, "You should hate each other for having let each other down."

Erin went on to explain that long before the product launch date, her team warned their bosses for months that they weren't in line with the launch date, and they listed several ideas about what they could do in order to have a successful launch. Their ideas were rebuffed by the higher-ups who decided they would stick to the original plan and launch date. When that launch failed, Steve Jobs berated them for not coming up with alternate ideas for the launch (before he told them they should hate each other).

But they had come up with alternate ideas. Jobs and his management team heard them but didn't heed what they said.

Still, my point is, brilliancy aside, Steve Jobs belted out outrageous, toxic bullying behavior.

The subtle workplace bully, on the other hand, is not quite as aggressive as the toxic boss. Their behavior can be described as *passive aggressive* or *slightly* aggressive. Some might be sociopathic. Also, the workplace bully can negatively affect people who don't report to him (such as other managers, vendors, and customers).

You might even say the workplace bully's moniker is, in fact, "passive aggression." Take the toxic, bully boss, tone him down a bit, and you have *a subtle workplace bully!*

There are a few qualities that a *toxic full-on bully boss* and a *subtle/bully-lite boss* have in common: Both of them make people feel uncomfortable, most people are unhappy working for them, and even the "full bully" belittles people in subtle ways from time to time.

Our workplace bully can be just as miserable to be around as a full-on bully boss. Plus, since the workplace bully's behavior is more understated, fewer people will see a workplace bully treat others with bad behavior. So, those on the receiving end of a workplace bully's treatment usually don't get the sympathy that others receive who work for a toxic boss. Workplace bullies don't yell at people and their behavior is not overt. They are more cunning and clever about how, when, and to whom they dole out their jerky ways.

Whereas people who work with or for a full/toxic bully more easily find others who are treated badly by him (and then find camaraderie with each other), people who work for a subtle workplace bully may not very easily find others who receive equal workplace bully treatment. Therefore, someone who works with or for a subtle workplace bully may feel isolated, as if they are the only person who has difficulty with him.

Meanwhile, the symptoms of a target of each type of bully can be the same.

SAME SYMPTOMS
Stress, can't sleep, headaches, etc.

TOXIC
BULLY

Other people
know

Others
sympathize

SUBTLE
BULLY

Hardly anyone
knows

You suffer
almost
anonymously

Here is an example of a situation with both a toxic boss and a bully-lite boss. Let's say an employee has an emergency with a family member and needs to leave work early. Once the employee makes it known that she needs to leave for the day for a family emergency, a toxic boss will rant about the employee's request, perhaps even putting the employee down. The workplace bully, on the other hand, will be more restrained in his response. He may say it's okay for the employee to tend to their family issue but will later use sarcasm, or he will be supportive of the employee *now* only to use the absence later as a "ding" to the employee at review time.

As a further example, Nancy worked for a builder in a Chicago suburb. She was married for 35 years, had three grown children, and had gone through a divorce one year earlier. She was still close to several of her ex-husband's relatives. She got a call that her ex-husband died suddenly of a heart attack and the family expected her to be at the wake and funeral. She received the phone call from her sister-in-law while she was at work, and she immediately told her boss that her ex-husband died and that she would need to have Thursday off to attend the funeral.

Her boss' response was, "Boy, you'll do anything to get a day off!"

Excuse me?

Notice that he didn't yell, stomp around, or berate her. Rather, he made a comment which showed a lack of sensitivity and he joked with her, but they didn't have a joking relationship with each other.

The workplace bully-lite is a *subtle* bully.

Is Your Boss or Colleague a Bully-lite?

In order to determine whether you're being bullied by a subtle, bully-lite character, look through the list of questions below. For each you will answer "yes" or "no." The first section relates to the potential bully. (Some of the questions and topics also appear in other parts of the book.) The second section relates to you.

Questions for People Who Might Work with a Workplace Bully

Questions Related to the Potential Subtle Bully:

1. Do you need to request your workplace bully to listen to you multiple times during a discussion?
2. Do you "think twice" about bringing up a topic for discussion with your bully?
3. When you are talking to your workplace bully, does he appear to be listening to you, but you wonder if he is simply thinking of the next thing he wants to say?
4. Does your bully work long hours? Is it because she is doing other peoples' jobs besides her own? (or instead of her own?) Or because she involves herself in minutiae?
5. When people "draw a line" for your bully, does he try to cross it?

6. Has your workplace bully made you or others feel fear?
7. Does your bully create an atmosphere of secrecy?
8. If so, does that secrecy lead to fear and then to mistrust?
9. Do you find that your level of work production drops because working with your workplace bully costs you a lot of energy?
10. Has your bully purposely not invited particular people to a meeting who should have been invited?
11. Does your bully make fun of people, either to their face or behind their back?
12. Has your workplace bully chosen to not speak to you (but she should and needs to) in favor of speaking to others?
13. Has your bully told you that people don't like working with you?
14. Have you ever felt that you needed to follow behind your bully with a "big broom" to clean up his messes?
15. Have you suspected your bully didn't tell his employees why he wanted them to do certain tasks because he doesn't trust them and he wants to see their detailed work?
16. Has your workplace bully ever made someone cry at work?
17. Has someone ever quit their job because they could not work with the bully?
18. Does your bully appear to be afraid to make decisions?
19. Does your workplace bully's communication of anger seem destructive (not constructive)?
20. Is your bully unwilling to "roll up his shirtsleeves" to help or unwilling to give you helpful ideas or advice?
21. Have you ever needed to find someone with more authority to communicate your messages with your bully because she refused to hear you?
22. Have you heard your workplace bully making excuses for his behavior by saying, for example, "I have to lead this project," or "This project has to get done on time"?

23. Has your bully twisted the facts of a situation to make her look better or to make you look worse (or both)?
24. Is there more than one bully at your company and they support each other in the bullying?
25. Has your workplace bully ever given his employees tasks to accomplish, and then later asked them why they did those tasks?
26. Does your bully tend to give people tasks that take up a lot of their time but don't have a high return, waste peoples' time, or waste the company's money?
27. Does your bully badger people with unnecessary questions, statements, email, etc?
28. When people ask your workplace bully a question, is he like a magician, pulling his answer out of his sleeve?
29. Does the bully blame others for poor communication, but in reality he is the poor communicator?
30. Has your bully made up (or embellished) stories about people in order to get his way?
31. Has your workplace bully frowned upon your choice or proposal to communicate with someone in senior management on your own?
32. Has your bully ever directed a verbal "mini blow up" at you?
33. If your bully has blown up at you, do you realize there was no negative repercussion for him or her?
34. Now that you're thinking of the workplace bully's negative repercussions of her bad actions toward you, do you realize she hasn't experienced any or very little? (i.e. she gets away with treating you badly)
35. Does your bully rarely accept your ideas, ignore your ideas, or put down your ideas?
36. When you've requested your bully to think strategically, does he choose instead to focus on tactical issues at a micro level?
37. Is your workplace bully so focused on achieving a goal that he doesn't care how badly people are treated on the way to the goal?

38. Does the culture at your workplace support (and even reward) subtle bullying behaviors?

Questions Related to You:

Have the behaviors of this person resulted in you experiencing any of the following:

1. Loss of sleep
2. Less ability to concentrate at work
3. Increased frequency of headaches
4. Increased frequency of other pain or ailments
5. Feelings of anxiety
6. Elevated blood pressure
7. Getting upset easily
8. Taking your upset feelings out on others (coworkers, family members, friends)
9. Feeling depressed
10. Low energy
11. Over eating or loss of appetite
12. Increased rate of hair loss
13. Increased drinking of alcohol
14. Other self-destructive behaviors
15. A sense of dread when you're on your way to work

Even if you answer "yes" to only a few questions, you probably have a subtle workplace bully in your life.

Since self-destructive behaviors are so injurious to you, I want to take a moment to cover them now. Self-destructive behaviors that stem from workplace bullying can include:

- Drinking too much alcohol
- Binge eating and other eating disorders
- Using drugs to cope
- Becoming addicted to drugs, alcohol, sex, gambling, shopping, etc.

- Obsessing about work deadlines to the point of feeling ill
- Deciding to appear incompetent at your work because you decide you can't complete it well anyway

Some of these self-destructive behaviors come to be from the inability to be assertive with your personal boundaries. Workplace bullies usually step all over a target's personal boundaries. If you find that is true for you, take care that you don't fall into these behaviors. Get professional help if you find you are moving toward, or are already in, a self-destructive emotional state.

So now what do you do if you work with or for a workplace bully?

- Should you look for another job?
- Should you hang in there and hope he changes?
- Is there anything you can do to get the person to change for the better?
- Should you even care? If so, why?

Maybe the workplace bully in your life is not your boss but is a coworker or client (or even an employee who reports to you). Working *with* them can be almost as draining as working for them.

Let's delve further into the psyche of the workplace bully and get to know this person better.

An Examination of Common Behaviors that Characterize Subtle Workplace Bullies

Bullies at work exhibit a variety of behaviors. Some described in this section will sound familiar to you.

Let's look at several types of bullies found in workplaces who can be considered as *subtle bullies* and examine some of their traits and behaviors.

The Subtle Workplace Bully Focuses on the Destination,
Not the Journey

I read a statement once that said, "Focus on the journey, not the destination." I realized that the workplace bully does the opposite: He focuses on the destination, not on the journey. By doing that, he misses opportunities along the way to build understanding and to build relationships.

When I read the statement, I had just been to lunch with a small group of people that included my workplace bully at the time. What occurred at our lunch actually highlighted a problem that the workplace bully has outside of work, but it related to his work as well.

At lunch, he talked about taking family vacations to visit relatives in Iowa. He and his wife have two young boys who were five and seven years old at the time. He said they make the drive in about seven hours, but that one time it took 10 hours because the kids wanted to eat and go to the bathroom "too often." He said before they had kids, he once made the drive in 5 ½ hours! He thought we would be impressed. Now that they have kids, and now that he knows he doesn't want the trip to last 10 hours, he makes everyone pile in the car before breakfast. His wife brings breakfast, lunch, snacks, and drinks. They make one stop for gas and the bathroom.

Someone at the table asked him if he gives his kids a "can."

He responded gruffly, "No, I don't give them *a can.*"

I turned to the person who asked the question and said, "A can to go to the bathroom in?"

Yes.

It's always nice when someone else teases your workplace bully. (The person teasing him also said, "If I tried that with my kids, they'd kill me.")

(I found out later that he really gave his kids a two liter bottle. I hope they had good aim!)

While thinking about this, I realized that the workplace bully's focus is on the goal. Getting to the goal as fast as possible, no matter what, is of utmost importance. The workplace bully's "goal mantra" could be: *It doesn't matter who you hurt on the way, as long as you reach your goal. Building relationships along the way doesn't matter, as long as you reach that longed-for goal.*

The problem with this "goal mantra" is that it leaves no room for staff development. It is during the process of getting to the goal that employees develop their career acumen, make mistakes, learn from those mistakes, and get guidance from a good leader/boss.

As I heard my colleague ask the workplace bully if he gave his kids a can to go to the bathroom for the long drive in the car, and then heard my colleague say how his own kids would kill him if he tried to do the same thing on a long car trip, the ridiculousness of forgetting the journey just to meet the goal quickly sunk into me: *This is yet another characteristic of some workplace bullies.* And occasionally, even his own family cannot escape his bullying ways.

Has your workplace bully ever been *so focused on an end result* that:

- He doesn't care about the nastiness that comes out of his mouth at his team....
- She isn't bothered by team members mistreating one another....
- He could care less how much overtime people are working....
- She gets irritated when people make mistakes rather than using it as an opportunity for learning and staff development....

...as long as you reach your goal on time?

The Subtle Workplace Bully is Too Busy Thinking of What She'll Say Next Than to Listen to You

There are people who appear to listen to others. However, when you're speaking they're not *really* listening, either because they're stubborn and believe they're right or because they're very self-centered. Instead, they're thinking of what they're going to say next. Even when you make a good point, they will not acknowledge it.

From Karen

Bob was a vice-president who took it upon himself to back-up a clerk who came to him with an issue. The clerk wanted the software system changed to accommodate her need. The change requested was complicated and costly to make. When I spoke to this clerk, she laid out the business case. I told her the business case was exactly what I needed, but in writing, and to please write up the business case in an email as she described it to me. She agreed to do that.

A few days later, she sent an email requesting the change, without writing the business case for it, and cc'd Bob (who was not her direct boss and was several layers up the org chart).

I replied, reminding her I had asked her to write up the business case she had stated in person in my office. At the end of the email, I wrote, "I'm not asking you to write a *full business case*, just the items bulleted above." (Simple business case items were bulleted and the words "full business case" were hyperlinked to an example of a full business case. She could see I was asking her for one small piece.)

After this, Bob got over-involved. When I met with him later, he said, "And you told her to write up a full business case and then linked to it." (Read that out loud in a snide tone of voice to get the gist of it.)

I said, "No, I didn't," and then pulled out a copy of the email. I laid it out on Bob's desk so that he could see it as I quoted it.

"It says, 'I'm *not* asking you to write a full business case, just the items bulleted above.'"

Did Bob reply, "Oh. I read that wrong"? No. He was too busy in his head thinking of what to say next.

Does your workplace bully appear to be listening while you're talking? When you finish and it's her turn to talk:

- Does she speak words that appear to show she ignored everything you just said?
- Do you wonder why you just wasted your breath?
- Do you feel bewildered?
- If there is another person in the room, do you feel a need to pull them aside to ask if you're the crazy one?

The Subtle Workplace Bully Complicates the Issues by Getting Unnecessarily Involved

Carol is a young analyst at a software company who coordinates with the Human Resources (HR) staff on payroll and benefits data. She thought a particular piece of the work belonged with HR. She had a good relationship with the vice-president of Operations, Nancy, and asked to speak with her to run an idea past her. While neither HR nor Carol reported to Nancy's organization, Nancy agreed to meet with her.

Carol laid out her ideas to Nancy for how the work was currently being done and how she thought a particular task should be handled by HR. Nancy agreed with Carol that her idea was a good one.

After the meeting, Nancy emailed the HR director, Keith, and copied Carol and Bob (the CFO and also Keith's direct boss and Carol's boss' boss) telling Keith that his team should handle the task as Carol suggested. Emails then flew back and forth between Keith and Nancy—many long, wordy emails. Bob finally had enough and said Carol would do the task.

Some bully-lite people get overly-involved in workplace issues when they would be better off letting go and not getting involved. They become an extra person in a situation, complicating things more than they need to be. Getting involved—when they should leave well enough alone or allow the people who really are involved to work it out themselves—is a bully-lite calling card.

This is called *triangulation*. Often occurring in dysfunctional families, a workplace bully will insert themselves into situations and triangulate the communication. Far from helping, this type of involvement is full of he said/she said commentary, unnecessary emails, misunderstandings, bad feelings, and innuendo that lead to increased mistrust and strained work relationships.

Often, workplace bullies (WBs) triangulate because they're convinced only *they* know how to do whatever the issue is and the people working with them are either not as smart or as competent as they are. Also, since they assume no one trusts them, they don't trust others, which leads them to try to control people and situations.

I have found that people who get involved in triangulation do so repeatedly. If you've ever heard stories from people who have dysfunctional family members, you'll find stories of frequent triangulation. Managers in the workplace who triangulate will waste your time! Some of them will even suggest that you're the person involved in the triangulation, not them. *How's that for dysfunction?*

In the story of Carol and Nancy, Carol has the right to go to whoever she wants to have that person be a sounding board. After Nancy listed to Carol, Nancy should have suggested that Carol request a meeting with Keith and Bob. Then Carol, Keith, and Bob could work together to arrive at a solution (leaving Nancy out of it). Handling the matter in this way, Nancy would have demonstrated leadership, coaching, and restraint. Instead, Nancy over involved herself and got into triangulation.

Following email (or other electronic communications) or conversations with your workplace bully, do you find yourself thinking:

- Why is she involving herself in this?
- His interjections aren't helping at all!
- We already had the right people involved. She's an extra person who is making the situation worse.

The Subtle Workplace Bully Won't Hesitate to Stab You in the Back

Most of us experienced being stabbed in the back in our teenage years. Regardless of the first time it happens to you, it's always a surprise. A person appears to have your best interests at heart, and then you find out they betrayed you in some way.

By the time you find out a workplace bully stabbed you in the back, quite a bit of damage may have already been done to your reputation. It will take some work on your part to clean it up.

From Sandy

When I started working at this company, we had three sections in my department and had five supervisors to manage everyone, which was about 30 employees, and a department manager, Rob, who was a pretty good manager.

About five years later, Rob chose to retire early. The company decided to give his job to someone from another department, Bill. I was familiar with Bill but didn't know him very well. Many other people at the company knew him, however, both professionally and socially. The company announced that Bill would get the manager's job about three weeks prior to Rob's retirement. After that announcement, two people came to me — separately — and both had the same thing to say. Each of them warned me, "Bill is a back stabber. Watch out for him."

By that time, our department had grown to 60 people. I figured with a 60-person department and a completely new department to manage and learn about, that should keep Bill busy enough to not become a back stabber for me.

Fast-forward about two years. I found out Bill had said negative things about me to two supervisors and Lord knows who else. He had no reason to say those things other than being a serial back stabber.

The people he said these things to didn't know Bill as a back stabber, so they took him at his word. (He hadn't stabbed them in the back at that point, anyway.) By then I had a different supervisor, too, who was bratty.

I ended up leaving the company a year later.

A stranger can't stab you in the back. The only people who can become back stabbers are those to whom you gave a certain amount of trust or, in the workplace, people who became colleagues who have at least a bit of work history with you.

Has your workplace bully ever:

- Done or said something with the intent to discredit you?
- Done or said something that resulted in other colleagues not wanting to work with you, changing their ideas about you, or having some new negative image of you?
- Brought up in conversation items in a review that were complete surprises to you or were not factually correct?

*The Subtle Workplace Bully is Disageeable Even When
Agreeing to Disagree*

Have you ever experienced someone disagreeing with
you, but doing it in a nice way? You leave the discussion—not
agreeing with each other—but no one's self esteem or honor
was reduced as a result of the disagreement.

On the other side of the coin, have you and another person
ever disagreed about some topic, and the two of you seem to
be agreeing to disagree, but you leave the discussion feeling
badly, with a piece of your self-worth missing or just some
"bad taste in your mouth" about how the conversation ended?

There is a difference between "agreeing to disagree,
agreeably" and "agreeing to disagree, *disagreeably*." The workplace bully may pat himself on the back for being the type of
person who *agrees to disagree*, but he does so in a *disagreeable*
manner.

I give the credit for this idea to my late friend, Richard,
who often taught people in his life the difference between
"agreeing to disagree, *agreeably*" and "agreeing to disagree,
disagreeably." Richard and I were like brother and sister and
we even fought like brother and sister. When we disagreed
about something, we didn't reduce the other person by cutting
the other down. We didn't belittle each other or the other's ideas.

Richard didn't want the people in his life to think that
someone else in their life—whether a spouse, boyfriend/girl-
friend, friend, or colleague—was being nice while disagreeing
on a topic when the other person was actually being destructive.

From Kurt

At a consulting job my company had at one point, one of
the directors at the company told me that one of my con-
sultants was doing his work too slowly. The people he was
working with wanted him to be replaced. I thought they
weren't giving him a chance.

When the director and I discussed it, we didn't completely agree about the situation or what to do about it.
While we disagreed, I didn't leave the discussion feeling
put down or that my ideas were put down.

In contrast, there was another manager at this company
who I had to work with regularly and who disagreed with
me on a regular basis. When I would leave discussions
with him, I sensed he subtly had put down my opinion. He
seemed like he was agreeing to disagree. But his way of
doing so was, well, destructive. It certainly wasn't constructive.

It was as if he was saying (without words), "I'll agree to
disagree with you. But for doing so, TAKE THAT! A-HA!"
(Fake knife stab wound here.)

Can you think of people in the past who have agreed to
disagree with you, but have done so agreeably? They've been
polite, pleasant, haven't set out to put you down for having a
different opinion, and haven't used passive aggression to punish
you in some way for not agreeing with them.

Likewise, can you think of people who have seemed to
agree to disagree with you, but they've done so disagreeably
(i.e. in a not-so-nice manner)? At first they might smile and
appeared to be polite, but they find ways to punish you or
belittle you for having a different opinion. Or they bring it up
over and over and just won't let it go. That is subtle bullying
behavior at its best!

The Subtle Workplace Bully Tries to
Buddy-Up with Other Employees

Someone who should be a leader by their title may actually
function as a *ringleader.* A ringleader has particular people on
his team for whom he gives a certain amount of political
protection (whether they are competent or not). When his
protected people make big mistakes, there won't be any negative

repercussions. He will become their buddy rather than their boss/leader. This is easier to see at after-hours activities or work parties where his direct-reports appear to be his buddies more than employees.

If you are not protected by this ring leader and have an issue with one of the people he protects, you will become his target. If you need his cooperation in order to be successful, you will have difficulty being successful at all.

Remember the story in the previous chapter from Janet, about her former boss, Brett? Brett was a ringleader. Brett rallied several people around him over time. Those were the people he protected and they protected him. He could behave in ways that brought him the laughs, but even if he belittled someone, he was protected enough so as not to get into trouble with anyone for it.

The people who rallied around him were also protected, even though at that point they hadn't treated anyone in a bullying fashion—yet.

This bullying situation can include socially marginalizing you. They find ways to not include you in the group, to make certain you're left out.

In this bully's mind, you are either on their team (and protected) or you are against them. There is no in between.

Has your workplace bully:

- Rallied some people around her?
- Chosen to protect certain individuals?
- Socially marginalized you, ensuring you're left out of situations?

The Subtle Workplace Bully's Anger is Destructive

Another trait of a workplace bully can be that the person handles their anger in a destructive manner rather than a constructive manner.

Researcher John Gottman identified four destructive forms of expressing anger that led him to be able to predict with over 90% accuracy whether a married couple will divorce. When I first heard about his research years ago I was mesmerized by his findings. I first heard it on a television news program. I remember my mouth dropped open as I listened. The first reason I was drawn to this news piece is because it's rare for any researcher to have such a high prediction success rate. The second reason was because I've observed over many years other people's anger destroying relationships. It was this research that pointed out it was their specific negative forms of expressing their anger that led to the destruction of their relationships, not the fact that they felt angry.[5]

Since then, I've studied some of his findings and realized the destructive forms of anger he identified that negatively affect marriages also negatively affect other relationships besides marriage.

Workplace bullies often express their anger in destructive ways. The four negative communication methods that John Gottman identified are:

- Contempt
- Criticism
- Defensiveness
- Stonewalling

When all four of these negative forms of communicating anger are present, relationships cannot survive. If three are present, the relationship will probably not survive. If one or two are present, relationships will be strained.

People who learn constructive ways to handle their anger will have happier and more successful relationships than people who hold onto one or more of the destructive forms.

To help wrap your thoughts around each of the four destructive forms of expressing anger, which is aimed at helping you to identify whether your workplace bully uses any of them, I'll briefly define each here.

Contempt

A workplace bully who uses contempt to express anger will be intent on insulting the other person. This can include statements such as, "You think you're so great," calling another person names, mean attempts at humor, mocking their target, and using their body language to express it such as by rolling their eyes, glaring, or showing disgust without using words.

You read a story earlier about a workplace bully using his sense of humor to bully another person. The use of mean humor is an example of a bully who has contempt for his target. The most subtle forms of contemptuous anger are the nonverbal facial expressions such as an eye roll or a quick half smile on one side of their face (as if they're thinking of calling you a name, they're just not saying it out loud).

Criticism

There is such a thing as constructive criticism, but a workplace bully doesn't use it. Rather, the criticism that comes out of him from a place of anger shows itself by going after his target's personality or character and usually involves blaming him as well. It can also involve "you always" statements, such as, "You always do…." or "You never do…." Really? Always? Never? This is not simply stating a complaint but making critical comments that go to the target's character.

At work, the anger-filled criticism can be in the form of saying, "You always do that report wrong," or "You're never on time." It could come in the form of blaming you for something going wrong when it's not completely your fault (or not your fault at all).

Defensiveness

If you've tried to speak with your workplace bully about his or her treatment of you, or about any other important issues, you may have encountered defensiveness. According to John Gottman, defensiveness can show itself in your workplace bully through denying responsibility for whatever it is you're trying to get him to see, making excuses for his behavior, pretending as if you have negative thoughts yourself ("negative mind reading"), making a secondary complaint to a valid complaint you raise, answering you by saying, "Yes, but …," repeating himself, and giving you a false smile.

In the workplace, a bully can display his anger by being defensive, justifying his use of bullying behavior when you attempted to discuss the fact that you don't want him to treat you in bullying ways (as if bullying you is an acceptable way to treat you). He might listen to a valid issue you bring up for conversation only to deny his responsibility for his part in it or by making a secondary complaint to trump your first complaint/issue.

Stonewalling

If your workplace bully gets to a point in a discussion where he doesn't reply to what you're saying, not even with a "Uh huh" and by his silence isn't working toward a constructive resolution, he is stonewalling. This is a type of silent treatment that communicates to his target that he disapproves. It is a destructive method of expressing anger.

At work, the bully who uses stonewalling when angry will dig in his heels and refuse to compromise when resolving an issue, he won't collaborate or support your plans, he won't be open to hear your side of the story, and he just refuses to cooperate.

Has your workplace bully used any of the destructive forms of expressing anger? Have you noticed:

- Contemptuous words or attitudes?
- Criticism that is not constructive?
- Defensive comments or actions?
- Your workplace bully stonewalling or giving you "the silent treatment"?

The Subtle Workplace Bully is Often Afraid to Make Decisions

While some subtle workplace bullies over inflate their egos and abilities, plenty of others are afraid their own abilities will fall short. This type of workplace bully will ask other people for ideas in order to slow down their decision making. This alone doesn't make them a workplace bully. Plenty of managers in new positions take some time to get to know their direct reports and colleagues and strive to have an inclusionary management style, gathering input from several people before making a decision.

The key to indecisiveness being a subtle bullying tactic is how it plays out later *and* whether the workplace bully continues to be indecisive after settling into her management role. After she finally makes a decision following gathering input and rationalizations from others, if the decision backfires or has even a mild downside, does she blame the others?

This workplace bully doesn't want to own her decisions or make a mistake. Rather than be *real* with her team and own a decision that didn't turn out well (compared to the 12 decisions that were good), she blames the poor outcome on other people.

One upper management person I know tells a story about being in a monthly meeting of senior managers (VP level and C level) at his company where one individual often prefaced what he said with, "I don't mean to be a jackass," and then continued to speak proving he actually is a jackass by blaming other people for decisions that didn't work well. This went on for several months. Finally at another monthly meeting, after this workplace bully said, "I don't mean to be a jackass," my friend said, "Stop. You tell us you don't want to be a jackass, and then you keep talking and show us you're a jackass. Either stop telling us you don't want to be a jackass (because you really do), or just stop being a jackass."

Everyone in the room laughed because they were all thinking the same thing. However, they had worked with this workplace bully for several years. No one stood up to him to confront his behavior until my friend confronted him at this meeting.

Has your workplace bully:

- Delayed making decisions time after time?
- Blamed others when decisions they made turned out badly?
- Feigned not wanting to be a jackass but then acted like a jackass?

The Subtle Workplace Bully Perpetuates Dysfunctional Behavior

If you don't have a dysfunctional family member, hearing a boss or colleague make dysfunctional statements or behave in dysfunctional ways can be a strange experience.

While meant to make you feel uncomfortable, let you know who is boss, and put you in your place, hearing dysfunctional words and phrases out of the mouth of a colleague can be something you don't even fully realize occurred until hours later.

Check the list below to see if any sound like something you've heard or seen before:

Bully Behavior:	Explanation:
"People don't like working with you," he says.	You ask, "Which people?" And then he won't tell you. Just "people." Could be one person. Could be no one. Could be just him.
Sending email after email, often text-dense, especially in situations in which he shouldn't be so involved.	These often include what I call "throw-up emails" where he barfs a bunch of words into an email and clicks "Send." It also typically involves the triangulation mentioned earlier.

Bully Behavior:	Explanation:
Telling you there is a problem with you but not telling the full story.	Someone has a bone to pick and you are the target. Dysfunctional workplace bullies love this and wallow in it. They will look for situations such as this in order to interject themselves to create problems and stress for you.
Misquoting you.	This is fun when they misquote you when you're right in the same room! It's more difficult when you find out they misquoted you, but not in your presence.
Giving certain people extra nice treatment while marginalizing you.	This shows itself in a lack of empathy for the socially-marginalized people (you!) and in ultra-empathy for a few chosen people.
Deliberately humiliating you.	She will find ways to humiliate you —usually in front of others or via email to multiple people. This is another form of socially marginalizing you. (It is also possible for the workplace bully to humiliate you when no one else is present.)
A refusal to see what is obvious to you.	This is a form of denial. If you point out anything negative about his behavior, he refuses to see it or acknowledge it.
Lack of healthy boundaries.	We all set healthy boundaries with people at work, such as, don't put me down, do give me the credit when I deserve it, don't stop me from communicating with particular people, don't over-involve yourself in my work. She will cross your healthy boundaries because she doesn't respect you.
Gets involved in conflicts and creates more conflict.	Rather than get involved to resolve conflicts constructively, his involvement creates more conflict. This behavior is destructive.

Bully Behavior:	Explanation:
Shaming you and turning words around.	There are WBs who never interrupt you while you're talking. Rather, they turn words around and find ways to shame you.
Creates an environment of fear.	When people feel fear in the workplace, they are usually afraid of a person—the workplace bully.
Attempts to control people or situations.	She tries to control people or details. This might include jealousy that isn't fitting to the situation.
Withholding resources from you.	The workplace bully might withhold a number of things: funding, people you need to meet with or speak to, supplies, access to information or systems, tools you need, etc. They withhold resources you need to succeed.
Creates an environment of secrecy.	You find out about something that was kept secret for a while. You wonder why it was secret. The secrecy seems to make people less trustful. The lack of transparency occurs often.

The Subtle Workplace Bully is Not a High Maintenance Manager

Another workplace character I've come across is the *high maintenance manager* and you might find them in the workplace, too. While they are not bullies, this person is stressful to work with but in a different way than subtle bullies. This is mainly because the high maintenance manager's behavior *does not contain malice.*

Here is an example:

Paul is a hard-working program manager who gets involved in a variety of projects at his company. He knows a lot about how the main software package works but he often drains the people working with him on the team.

During meetings, Paul will often take time to figure out how to work with downloaded data and will make people sit there as he tries a variety of ideas to get the data and files to work. While most people would figure out that type of work while at their own office and not at a meeting, Paul has others wait for him...and watch. If anyone objects or suggests they end the meeting and reconvene later, Paul gets upset.

Paul is a lot of work for others and causes others to have increased stress. He doesn't display the behaviors of a workplace bully but he is regularly *high maintenance.*

People who are high maintenance cause stress for others around them. They do so without demeaning anyone, so they're really not bully-lite. *While this book is not about high-maintenance people, it's important to know that these people also exist in the workplace and can cause you stress.* They are easier for you to manage than a workplace bully.

	High Maintenance Manager:	Workplace Bully:
Her attitude	Does not contain malice.	Contains malice
How does he treat others?	Doesn't demean others or belittle others	Demeans others, belittles others, etc.
Will she apologize?	Yes	No
Causes you stress?	Yes	Yes
Will he get angry?	Yes	Yes
Is his anger destructive?	No	Yes
Will she get overly-involved?	Maybe, but not to intentionally triangulate	Maybe, but to triangulate

The Subtle Workplace Bully is Not Necessarily a Narcissist

Narcissists are a particular subset of bullies. While they often start off getting to know you by being charming and attractive, within a certain amount of time your encounters with them will lead to an increase in your stress level.

When you look at the character traits and behaviors of narcissists, you'll see words and phrases that should look familiar by now as we get toward the end of this chapter because many of their behaviors in the workplace are the same as the bully behaviors about which you've already read. Characteristics and behaviors of narcissists include being self-centered, argumentative, manipulative, opportunistic, exaggerators, and arrogant.

In the workplace, narcissists are usually overly-focused on being successful and powerful. They become jealous of others quite easily, although their jealously in the workplace won't necessarily stand out as actual jealousy. They're more likely to act out their jealous thoughts by doing many of the bullying actions described in this book. For example, their jealousy could lead them to badger a person with questions or put down someone's ideas. Their jealously might be displayed as a sense of entitlement at work, such as being entitled to pro- motions, pay increases, and plum assignments over equally deserving colleagues.

Some narcissists keep workaholic type hours and have a penchant for perfection. Many have delusions of grandeur and express their ideas of their own greatness when talking with others. They have a strong need for admiration and will look for praise from other people.

Narcissists might continually say that tasks are being completed but, in truth, those tasks are not getting done at all (certainly not on schedule). At the same time, another hall- mark of narcissists is that they will take credit for work other people did. They will put down their boss and others they report to (even though the put-down isn't warranted), often by saying their boss doesn't have the credentials to lead and *they* should have the boss' job.

To someone with limited access to him who only casually observes him, the narcissist will appear to be overly-confident and arrogant. But beneath it all, he is actually lacking in confidence and is hypersensitive to criticism.

The one characteristic narcissists exhibit that separates them from others is a lack of empathy for other people.

Empathy is defined as the ability to feel what another person is feeling and experiencing, as in "putting yourself into the other person's shoes." The Merriam-Webster Dictionary defines empathy as "The action of understanding, being aware of, being sensitive to, and vicariously experiencing the feelings, thoughts, and experience of another of either the past or present without having the feelings, thoughts, and experiences fully communicated in an objectively explicit manner; *also*: the capacity for this."

You may have experienced what the other person is going through or you may have not experienced the same thing, but if you have empathy for them, you can imagine what they are going through even if you haven't experienced the same yourself. Empathy is similar to sympathy, but sympathy involves the *recognition* that the other person is going through an experience, not necessarily *feeling the same thing* and *knowing how they feel.*

For example, my father died when I was a young adult. For another young adult whose father dies, I have empathy for them because I've gone through the same thing. As another example, I've never had cancer, but because I can imagine what someone is experiencing who has cancer and feel for them, I have empathy for that person.

A narcissist doesn't feel empathy for anyone. A narcissist in the workplace would display a lack of empathy for a colleague by not caring that the colleague is healing from surgery, has a sick child, had a death in the family, has too many tasks on their to-do list and can't get them all done on time and with excellence, and the list goes on. They can't feel for other people and other people's pain. They will often first show their lack of empathy for another person when that person disagrees with him.

While narcissists in the workplace will be bullies 99% of the time (even in subtle ways), very few workplace bullies are narcissists.

I've known plenty of workplace bullies who could show empathy to others—just not to the people they were bullying at the time they were bullying them. I was once shown empathy by someone who wasn't a bully who then became a bully a year later. When she became a bully, she displayed the following behaviors that are also the behaviors of a narcissist: Into power for herself (by keeping secrets from others), manipulation (she changed a story around to make herself look better), argumentative, and a sense of entitlement (she felt she was entitled to know more about the goings-on at the company than other people should know—connected to the secret-keeping). She was also involved in triangulation (although that is not necessarily a narcissistic trait). She did not, however, have a lack of empathy for others. I had seen her display empathy for other people in the months prior to her showing bullying characteristics.

When there is a narcissist in the office, as long as people know him and haven't just met him, 99% of those people will know there is something wrong with his behavior. Even if they are not a target (yet), if you are the target of a narcissist, the other people around you will probably support you in some way.

Bullies who are *not* narcissists are much more capable of hiding in the workplace and often only you (the target) will know they are a bully. This is why subtle bullying can be potentially more damaging to the target than bullying by a narcissist—everyone else thinks your subtle bully is a great person. What in the world is wrong with you? She's such a nice person. It must be all in your head!

Being the target of a subtle bully can be lonely if you're the only target and/or no one else sees how the bully treats you. When a narcissist is in the workplace, usually they will bully more than one target—usually several people become their target.

Meanwhile, be aware of the definition of a narcissist. They are in some workplaces and they will drain you of energy, confidence, time, and your health. But most workplace bullies are much more subtle than workplace narcissists!

Have You Identified Your Subtle Workplace Bully?

So far, have you identified the behaviors and traits of your bully boss or colleague? As you read parts of this chapter, did you think I was writing about *your* workplace bully?

Some people have told me about workplace bullies in their work history noting that, at the time, the bullying was so subtle they couldn't identify it as bullying. But later, looking back, they recall feeling a high level of stress and even wondering if they were the crazy person in the story. Now they realize they were being bullied in a "lite" fashion.

Furthermore, they tell me they wish they had a resource like this book or someone to talk to at the time to help them:

1. Identify the bullying behaviors of the other person
2. Figure out an action plan to deal with it
3. Get encouragement and support to take action

At this point, we're at step 1 in the list above where you are identifying the bullying behaviors of your workplace bully. Use a pen, a highlighter, whatever you want to make notes and identify the particular behaviors of the bully in your life.

In later chapters you will get to steps 2 and 3 when you will come up with an action plan for dealing with the workplace bully and get the encouragement and support you need to live out your action plan.

The workplace bully actually costs the company more money in the long run (and sometimes in the short run). Next, we will explore why it's unwise to keep workplace bullies on the payroll—much less in leadership.

If you choose to approach management or an executive at your company to help you with a bullying situation, arming yourself with the data in the next chapter will give you the information they'll want to know before they choose to help you. They usually care most about issues that negatively affect company profits.

3

Workplace Bullies are Bad for Business

"Treating people well and authentically respecting them does lead to far better business performance. We proved it works."

—Jerome Dodson, President, Parnassus Investments

Who should really care if a workplace bully is on staff at your company?

Well, researchers have tied costs to having bullies on staff, mainly by looking at lost productivity related to the stress they cause and also related to how much it costs to replace a trained employee who quits because they were bullied.

When you're the target of a workplace bully, you typically will not care a whole lot what it costs the company to keep them on staff. You just want them to stop their behavior. Or you want them to find a new job. In short, you want relief from the stress.

Arm Yourself with Financial Data

If you decide to talk to someone at your company about your experiences being bullied, it will be best if you have financial data to back-up your position that allowing bullying to exist in the workplace is financially bad for business. Some people at your company will care that you're having a stressful, negative experience due to the bad behavior of a boss or colleague. However, most people won't care at all.

The trigger that most of them will care about is that your bad experience with your workplace bully costs the company money in the form of higher expenses, lower sales, or both.

Arm yourself with the financial information in this chapter so that, if discussions about the bullying go further, you're ready to give more concrete reasons why workplace bullies are bad for business.

What is the Cost to the Company, Anyway?

Costs to the company to keep a workplace bully on staff can take a few forms, mainly:

- The stress caused by a workplace bully to the people they target means it takes the targets longer to be successful and to get work done.
- When people can't take working with the workplace bully any longer, they leave the company, taking their talent and knowledge with them. It costs money to replace them.
- HR may need to bring in a coach or consultant to work with a workplace bully, and that costs money.

In chapter 1 we looked at the most frequent symptoms in those of us dealing with a bully at work. They include anxiety, loss of concentration, lack of sleep, hypervigilance, headaches, and frequent illness. If we are not at our best when we go to work, this is a cost to the company of keeping a bully on staff.

Two researchers, Charlotte Rayner and Loraleigh Keashly, discovered how much it costs, on average, to keep a bully on staff when it means that the targets of bullies leave the company. First, they found that, on average, 15% of employees at a company experience some type of bullying from bosses, coworkers, and others. If there are 1,000 employees at a company, then, on average, 150 of them are bullied in some way every year.[6]

Of the people who are bullied, 25% leave the company because of it. Rayner and Keashly found that the cost to replace each employee is typically 20% to 30% of their annual salary. So let's say, on average, it costs $30,000 to replace an employee.

Getting back to our example of a company that has 1,000 employees, 150 of whom are being bullied, 25% (or 38) leave the company on average per year. At a cost of $30K to replace, that comes to $1.14 million annually.

Company has:	1,000 Employees
15% are being bullied:	150 Employees
25% of those bullied quit annually:	38 leave the company annually
Average cost to replace is $30,000 each (38 x $30,000):	Cost = $1.14 million per year to replace bullied employees

Besides the targets themselves, each target also has, on average, two people who witness the bullying. In our example, if 150 people are bullied per year at a company, an average of 300 people witnessed the bullying. Of those witnesses, 20% of them also leave the company at the same cost per person. This adds $1.8 million to the cost to replace them.

Two witnesses per bullied employee:	150 x 2 = 300 witnesses
20% of witnesses quit annually:	60 witnesses leave the company
Average cost to replace is $30,000 each (60 x $30,000):	Cost = $1.8 million per year to replace witnesses

The total cost of keeping bullies on staff equals $2.94 million annually for a company with 1,000 employees. ($1.14 million for departed targets + $1.8 million for departed witnesses.)

> In contrast, when people aren't bullied and don't witness bullying, Rayner and Keashly's research found that about 5% leave a company annually.

I'm not even mentioning the cost of time spent by other employees (the bully's bosses, the Human Resources department, etc.) to try to get the bully to stop their behavior (sometimes they don't try anyway).

Truly, the personal stress of being the target of a workplace bully is enough for me, cost to the company notwithstanding.

By the way, why should company executives care if they have a workplace bully on staff?

The costs, as shown above, will mount over time as their workplace bully continues to choose new targets. Most of these bullies will not stop or reform. I hope some of them will. But most will not.

Let's say you have no authority to fire your workplace bully. While it's nice to know that your workplace bully costs the company money (and perhaps more than you thought it did), you still need to look out for yourself and figure out what you want to do. You know you cannot go on working with this person indefinitely if his behavior stays the same. What is your hope?

In the next chapter, we'll review your options.

- Should you stay at the company?
- At what point should you begin looking for a new job?
- If you choose to stay, how can you do that without losing your health and your mind?

"Younger Women Ain't Gonna Take It"

Reading about women in the workplace in the second half of the 20th century, stories abound about women being mistreated from 1950 to 1980. Things got better for women in the '80s, with a smaller percentage claiming to be bullied or sexually harassed, but things were still not great.

As of this writing, though, when this book is being published, many women graduating from college in 2015 grew up being involved in competitive sports and being told they were as good as the boys in many pursuits. The women in this class are much more used to standing up for themselves and have been trained to do so since they were young children.

Research performed by the Workplace Bullying Institute in 2014 showed that 60% of workplace bullying targets are women.[7]

As each new year adds new employees in their early 20s to the workforce, each new graduating class of women expects to be treated better and more fairly than the women before them ever dreamed possible.

During my internship with a public accounting firm years ago, I witnessed my first experience of sexism in the workplace. Actually, I was quite appalled by something a manager said about a female employee who wasn't in the room. I had not experienced such statements by men in previous jobs or in school. I didn't confront the behavior of this manager at all. I was not the only person in the room, but I was the only woman in the room at the time he made this particular comment. No one mentioned that what the manager had said was inappropriate, so I assumed this was acceptable behavior in the workplace.

Barbara Walters told a story about early in her career when a manager chased her around his desk in his office. While she also was appalled, she didn't confront the behavior because it was accepted.

The women coming into the workforce in the 21st century do not expect to be treated with such sexism by anyone, much less by workplace bullies. We all need to get on board with this. A smaller percentage of this current group of younger women will tolerate bad behavior from bosses. The current group will be bolder than their predecessors. They will go to their Human Resources department for help, they will talk with their work peers about their problem boss, they will make an issue out of it, and/or they will quit. As time moves on, women are less and less likely to quietly deal with (or quietly tolerate) bosses who are bullies. The passive women who were more likely to silently tolerate bullying behavior from their bosses were the pre-baby boomers, baby boomers, and the early Generation-X-ers. Later Gen-X-ers, women born after 1975, are just not putting up with bad boss behavior in the same percentages as the women before them. And it's about time!

Be ready for this shift. These women were told over and over throughout their childhood and teen years that they were just as good as the boys at all kinds of activities. Don't be surprised when these women stand up for themselves in the workplace and demand to be treated with dignity and respect. Additionally, they grew up participating in sports that were not widely available when I was a kid. The sports experiences and coaching they received gave them life skills regarding competition and standing up for themselves.

The other shift that has occurred is in the women who are bullies; most of them target another woman instead of a man. Still, I believe that as the boomers and Gen X-ers move toward retirement, less women who are targeted for bullying will stick around in their jobs. They will leave and the company will have to spend money to replace them.

The Millennial generation of women, and the generations to follow them, won't stick around and "take it" like the women before them did. After they're fully trained and the company has invested in getting them up-to-speed, younger women who have a workplace bully for a boss or colleague (and who don't feel heard when they attempt to speak out) will find a new job, and the company will have to spend more money to find and train her replacement.

Performance and Interpersonal Skills
are Equally Important

In the first chapter, you read about how at some companies the bullying behaviors of some employees are ignored because they are high-performing employees. At those companies, the executives value employees with a high sales record, for example, more than they value how those employees treat their colleagues and direct reports.

While these bully employees exceed company targets, their interpersonal skills stink. If they're very subtle with their bullying, it's likely some people will think their interpersonal skills are fine, while their targets and witnesses know otherwise. It's going to take individual corporate leaders, business owners, and board members drawing a line in the sand and looking at high performing employees' full spectrum of behaviors in the workplace in order for this to change for the better.

I'd like to see a two-part year-end review on subtle bully employees that looks much like a child's elementary school report card, where the interpersonal skills count just as much as workplace performance. It might look something like this:

Bobby Smith's Year-End Review			
Work Performance		Interpersonal Development	
Exceeds sales quotas	A	Works well with others	D
Relationships with customers	A	Encourages colleagues to do well	C-
Stays within the department budget	B+	Doesn't triangulate	D
Collections: his/her customers pay on time	A-	Supports a fear-free workplace	C
Completes projects on time	A	Macro-mgr; doesn't involve self in minutiae	C-

The interpersonal development side on the right should be just as important as the work performance on the left!

I think the bully's year-end review should look more like this:

Jane Doe's Year-End Review			
Work Performance		Interpersonal Development	
Creates messes that others clean up	A	Works well with others	D
Takes credit for others' work	A	Encourages colleagues to do well	C-
Creates crises that only he/she can solve	B+	Doesn't triangulate	D
Shifts blame from self to others	A-	Supports a fear-free workplace	C
Undermines trust	A	Macro-mgr; doesn't involve self in minutiae	C-

The Consequences of Keeping Bullies on Staff

Most of the time, companies that keep bullies on staff will continue to have an uncontrolled amount of money going out the door while that person works at their company.

A senior partner of a law firm went through six administrative assistants in a year and a half, and he caused so much stress by bullying another senior partner that she abruptly quit after enduring his bullying to the point of losing weight and some hair. The workplace bully didn't bring in any more business than any other attorney on staff, so it wasn't clear why the owner/partners kept him on. In these cases, we can only guess why he isn't gone. Did he know something about one of the owner/partners (such as an affair) and threaten to tell if fired? We'll probably never know.

While I was at a client's office years ago where a workplace bully caused problems for me, the workplace bully got an offer from another company, but the present company countered the offer and he accepted. I, of course, thought the company was unwise to do that. I found out that this particular workplace bully had displayed these behaviors to a variety of women during his tenure at the company. I will tell you more about this story in a later chapter, as I didn't take his behavior but fought it on two fronts. It actually had a good ending.

Next, we will review your options. We'll review several coping strategies, help you decide whether you want to confront the bully (and how to do that), and help you to know when it is time to find a new job. Even if you feel you need to change jobs, enlisting new coping mechanisms now will help to reduce your stress level.

4

Caution: Bully at Work!– What Now?

They jeer, using words to kill; they bully their way with words.
They're full of hot air, loudmouths disturbing the peace.
People actually listen to them — can you believe it?
Like thirsty puppies, they lap up their words."

—The Message, Psalm 73: 8-10

I've had my share of workplace bullies throughout my career. Some have been bosses, some have been coworkers, and others have worked at my clients' offices.

Several years ago, after a day of being exhausted by a workplace bully at a client, I came home and just laid down on my living room floor. I didn't move until my dog came by to nudge me to get up. I know that these WBs can be draining emotionally and physically. They can suck the creativity out of you as if they're some life-sized workplace bully vacuum.

Working with them leads to increased stress, which is detrimental to your physical health, emotional health, and overall well-being. Remember the four outcomes of coaching? The workplace bully will destroy your well-being at the job, your competence, your sense of purpose, and if you work with him for too long, he'll also destroy your ability to have clear awareness. In the end, your work performance will suffer.

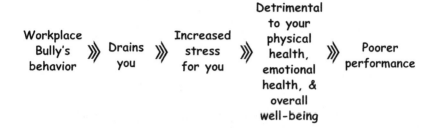

How to Manage a Workplace Bully

Have you ever heard of "managing up?" This is a learned skill you apply toward managing the person you report to. You can also use it to manage other WBs you don't report to.

How can you learn to manage your workplace bully so that you can cope with this person and enjoy your work life?

Even if you decide to look for a new job, you need to manage this part of your life in the meantime.

Are You Smarter Than a Workplace Bully?

You probably are smarter than most WBs. So you're going to have to pull out all of your smartness, set emotions aside as much as you can, and make some determined changes.

In fact, if the emotional side of what you've been experiencing with the workplace bully makes it difficult to concentrate on any of this, you're going to need to work extra hard to set the emotions aside temporarily to make a plan as you read the rest of this chapter. It may help to imagine yourself placing all of those emotions in a box, placing a lid on the box, and then setting the box somewhere out of the way. If that doesn't work as you try it by yourself, find someone to talk through it with you (you talk, they listen and possibly speak a bit to help you sort it through). You don't need the other person to help you solve the problem; you just need for them to listen so that you can pull those emotions away from you long enough for you to successfully work through your course of action.

Who should this person be? Probably someone who *doesn't* work at the company. A friend, a former colleague, or someone who is good at being a sounding board are good choices.

Three Options for Your Course of Action

I believe you have three possible options in dealing with the workplace bully and your situation:

1. Stay at the company, learn and apply coping mechanisms, and do nothing to end the workplace bully's bully-lite behaviors.
2. Stay at the company and work toward getting the workplace bully to change.
3. Change jobs: Leave the company or change departments at the same company.

Next, I will outline how each of the three options will work.

Option 1: Stay at the Company, Cope, and Do Very Little to Motivate the Bully to Change

While not my favorite choice of the three, staying at the company, figuring out a way to cope, but doing little to motivate the workplace bully to change is still an option. Maybe the effort it would take to work toward getting the workplace bully to change isn't a viable alternative for you right now. And even if you started a job search today, it could take a long time to find a new job.

So what does this option mean for you?

It suggests you'll work toward developing coping strategies only. This is a type of "survival mode" that will get you through each day and each week that you have to work with the workplace bully. In other words, by "do nothing else to change the workplace bully," I mean that you will not work toward getting the workplace bully to change her behavior, but you will change some things about yourself—namely, you will adopt strategies to make the best of the situation.

Create Distance: "Here's the Line"

You can create a tactic that keeps as much distance as possible between you and your workplace bully.

When I was a kid, we took a lot of vacations by car. These vacations were with my father after my parents divorced, and I had two younger brothers. The older of the two was an instigator. He constantly crossed boundaries with our youngest brother (and sometimes with me). When either the youngest or I were in the back seat with him, we used our hand to "draw" an imaginary line down the middle of the seat and tell him, "This is the line. Don't cross it!" We only created that "rule" after being poked, prodded, and taunted by him. My father got so tired of his instigations that he finally bought a cooler for snacks and put it in the middle of the back seat to create a more solid "line." Since the youngest was most often the recipient of the line-crossing and taunting, after a while my father made certain that one of the boys sat in the front passenger's seat and the other sat behind the driver's seat, making them "kitty-cornered" in the car (which meant I sat in the rear passenger's seat). When I got my driver's license and took a turn to drive, my father sat in the rear passenger's seat, keeping the boys as far apart from each other as possible. Having this "line" in place kept "Mr. Instigator" in check.

Likewise, you need to create some distance between you and the workplace bully. He's a "line-crosser," and he's been getting away with it for too long! Since you can't call on big daddy to "put a cooler" between you and Mr. or Ms. Workplace Bully, you need to take the matter into your own hands.

In this technological age, it's more and more possible to do business by distance. For example, instead of attending meetings in person, attend by conference call, thereby lowering the amount of time you spend in person with the workplace bully. Many companies use the services of a teleconferencing center, which provides toll-free numbers and a code that you give everyone attending the conference call. If your company doesn't want that expense, there are also free teleconferencing services available that give you a toll phone number and a code—all you pay for is the minutes on your own phone. In addition, Skype and other similar online services are free for group audio calls.

More companies provide their employees with laptop computers and a direct way to get their email remotely (as well as access to other company systems). You can work from just about anywhere. If your workplace bully is opposed to this manner of working (as many WBs are), find out who at your company supports remote work, which departments are doing this successfully, and then figure out a way to get support for telecommuting for your department (and especially for yourself). Even if you start with telecommuting one day a week, it's an improvement.

Can I Get a Witness?

Make certain that when you are around your workplace bully at least one other person is present. Witnesses are great! The less often the workplace bully can say something to you without anyone else around, the better.

One of my former WBs was at a client's office. In order to follow protocol, I really needed to treat him to lunch at the holidays. I invited another consultant who was working through my company. I also invited a fourth person from the client's company who was involved in the project I was working on and who actually was instrumental in getting me on the current project. When I called to ask the fourth person if he would like to join us for lunch, he asked, "Do you want me to be the chaperone?" He was joking, but I responded, "Yes, that would be great. Thanks!" Having another person present whenever you're with the workplace bully is a good thing.

I did not want to be alone with that workplace bully! I did not trust him. It was always better to be in his presence if there was at least one other trustworthy person with us. "Any person" would not do as the reliable second person, by the way! This particular workplace bully had three people around him who were "on his side," so to speak, and to whom he did not delve out jerky behavior. To have one of those people with him and me was just like cloning him. That's double trouble! Rather, I needed a cadre of trustworthy people to select from to be available and present in the room whenever I was around him.

Select a few reliable people and keep their names in the back of your mind. In fact, even if you don't know someone very well, and as long as they're not the workplace bully's buddy, a work acquaintance will do. Try to have at least one of these people around when you're with the workplace bully. It will help to have a witness if your workplace bully pulls something on you —at least someone to whom you can say afterward, "What was *that*?" Better yet, a witness in your presence may mean that the workplace bully will behave himself and won't pull anything at all. Either way, your stress level from being around him should be reduced from having a trustworthy person in the room.

Document Everything

Write down every conversation with the workplace bully as well as you recall. Type it into Word (or whatever application you use). Do not keep this document on your work PC. Get a flash drive and keep the file on it so that you can write about conversations as soon as possible. When you leave your desk or office, remove the flash drive from your PC.

If your workplace bully sends you emails that are good evidence, save those emails to your flash drive, too, in a folder created specifically for their emails.

When you write about conversations and situations with your workplace bully, your writing is likely to be emotional. That is okay. If the time comes later when you need to give documentation to someone, you can create "version 2" where you will smooth out the emotions in the writing to ensure it states facts without getting too emotional. You will keep "version 1," which is the original writing with raw emotions, just for yourself.

Some targets of bullies have told me they delayed documenting conversations and issues with their workplace bully, *and* they believe they won't forget any details when they later document what occurred. That isn't accurate! The longer you wait to create the documentation the more details and nuances you will forget.

Document your "version 1" as soon as possible. Then later, go back to re-read your "version 1" and create "version 2" from it.

The late Tim Fields, who wrote a lot about workplace bullying prior to his death, suggested when meeting with the workplace bully that you request to make an audio recording of the meeting. If they protest, it is probably because they want to create notes of your meeting by leaving out important details. By recording your meetings, you can quote people exactly and hear the tone of their voice. The most convenient way to record a meeting is through a recording app on your cell phone.

Having your notes in writing will protect you in the future if your bully gets worse. Also, the process of writing these things that happened will help you keep your sanity.

Learn to Pull Away Emotionally

As you develop some coping techniques, finding ways to emotionally pull yourself away from the workplace bully will help to keep you from being pulled down by this person. Several ideas in this section will help you do that.

Practice Detached Concern

Have you ever wondered how certain types of doctors and nurses cope with having a lot of sad cases of sick patients? For example, imagine being a pediatric oncologist. You would see and relate to all kinds of patients and their families, including kids who survive cancer the first time around, those who survive it after a fierce battle, and those whose cancer takes their lives. With all of the heartbreaking moments and days, how do these medical professionals do it day after day, and then have a normal life after work without emotionally falling apart?

I once knew a judge who heard cases of domestic violence all day, every day. Then at the end of each day, she came home to be with her own family. The stress of the sad stories she heard all day didn't affect her once she removed the black robe and left her chambers. How did she do it?

Many people in these types of careers practice "detached concern." This is a type of coping strategy that allows them to show they care about their patients while working with them, and then it allows them to emotionally pull away from the sadness of the situation later. This approach allows them to go on with their lives and keeps the emotion of the situation from negatively affecting everything else.

How can you cope with working with your workplace bully by practicing *detached concern*?

Psychologists often work toward helping their clients change their thoughts about a situation as a successful coping strategy (depending on the type of situation, of course). Imagine you're going to be able to do this: Change your thoughts about the workplace bully in your life so that she doesn't affect your work performance or your life negatively. In order to change your thoughts about the workplace bully so that you can cope with her in the workplace day in and day out, you will re-set your expectations about her, eliminate any self-blame you have about the situations you've been in with her in the past, view any difficulties with her as temporary situations, and re-learn how to "not care" how she behaves.

Let's break that down.

Learn How to "Not Care" about the Bully's Behavior

Picture yourself as the oncologist who works with emotional situations all day and must become detached from all of those situations at the end of the work day in order to live a normal life without loads of stress. In fact, picture yourself as that doctor who must practice *detached concern* each time he or she walks out of any examination room or hospital room.

Talk to a few doctors and ask them what it means to them to practice *detached concern* with their patients. What can you borrow from what they do and apply to your own life?

If you can learn how to not care about how your workplace bully acts and responds to you, you will save yourself a lot of heartache and headache.

Below are a few examples to contrast a stressful response to a workplace bully vs. a "not caring" response:

The Bully's Action	How the Target Reacts that is Stressful	How the Target Could React with "Not Caring" or "Detached Concern"
The workplace bully sends you another email nit-picking about something.	Click "Reply" and write a response. Click "Send."	Close the email. Don't reply. Save the email in a separate folder on a flash drive to refer to later if/when you need to refer to the workplace bully's behavior.
The workplace bully socially marginalizes you at meetings.	Arrive at the meeting early. Try to participate in discussion during the meeting. Stay at the meeting an extra minute or two to be involved in the post-meeting conversations.	Arrive at the meeting just on time. Listen but don't actively participate in the meeting. If other people check their phone during the meeting, then do that, too. Leave the meeting as soon as it's over.
The workplace bully gives you a dirty look (or refuses to acknowledge your presence) when you pass her in the hallway or other workplace spot.	Over-think what you should do. Wonder what that was about. Think about it for the next 30 minutes.	Laugh. Even laugh out loud. Shake your head. Then say to yourself, "Life is too short for this."

Reset Your Expectations

In the last 15 years, I can think of several conversations I've had with colleagues and friends who told me about a difficult person in their lives who consistently proved to be jerky or a bully in one way or another. Sometimes these stories involved a boss or coworker; other times it involved a relative or friend. In all of these conversations I'm referring to, my colleague or friend had an expectation for a particular type of behavior from the other person in their story.

Also in all of these accounts, my colleague or friend expected the other person to behave in ways in which that person was *never* going to behave. So my colleague or friend would end up feeling frustrated, disappointed, or angry (or a combination of the three) when the person we were discussing behaved questionably.

I pointed out to these people that they had set an expectation *inside themselves* for the other person, and it was an expectation that the other person was most likely never going to meet. After letting that thought sink in for a few seconds, I asked, "Wouldn't it be better *for you* if you reset your expectations for what Jane will do rather than consistently expect her to choose to respond to you in a way that she will never do?" And then, again, I would let that thought sink in for a few seconds.

If you expect your workplace bully to act in his outrageous ways, you might not be so surprised when it happens. It doesn't make his behavior okay; it just lessens some of the shock on you.

What about you and your workplace bully? Have you expected him to respond in ways more befitting a respectable manager? Perhaps he just doesn't have the ability to be a respectable manager! It's time to re-set your expectations about how he will respond in any given situation.

Think about some of the jerky ways your workplace bully has responded to you over the past month. For any of those situations that caused you to feel stressed, frustrated, disappointed, or angry, put your state of mind back to just before he responded in a bullying manner. Imagine yourself back at that time resetting your expectation for his response at that very moment, and reset it *to expect* the type of response he actually gave. Next, you got his jerky response. A-ha! He met your expectation right on the mark! Bingo!

Now comes the more difficult part. You will have encounters with your workplace bully over the coming weeks. He will have the opportunity to respond to you again. What will your expectation be of his words and actions? Will you reset your expectations of him now to include *bullying responses?* And in the rare moment he responds to you as if he were a normal, respectable manager, woo-hoo! He exceeded your expectations!

On the table below are a few examples of typical workplace situations, listed in the first column. If you were dealing with a normal person instead of a workplace bully, the congenial behavior of someone who isn't a bully is in column 2. This highlights what your normal expectation would be for civilized people.

But your bully doesn't behave in civilized ways. His responses and actions are not necessarily agreeable and harmonious. His typical response to the situation is noted in column 3.

The Situation:	Your Normal Expectation is:	Reset Your Expectation To:
#1: You send the workplace bully an email.	He reads the email. He doesn't understand it. He replies and politely asks for clarification of A, B, & C.	Expect he reads the email. He doesn't understand it. Then he either clicks "reply" or stops by your desk to blame you for being so confusing in your email. (And you get his emotional stuff. Anger. Blow up. Red face. Or even subtle blame.)

The Situation:	Your Normal Expectation is:	Reset Your Expectation To:
#2: You're leading a meeting of 12 people and your workplace bully is there. Someone asks a question that you're prepared to answer.	As the leader of the meeting, you answer the question. Others might comment and participate in the discussion. No one attempts to take over the leadership of the meeting.	Expect the workplace bully to begin talking and then take over leadership of the meeting. (If the meeting is in person, he might also stand up and/or go to the front of the room.) This is embarrassing to you as the real leader of the meeting. Expect to be embarrassed.
#3: You invite 10 people to a regularly scheduled bi-monthly meeting, including the workplace bully. In this situation, the meeting is today.	She attends the meetings and participates with the others in conversation, sharing information, and reaching shared goals.	Expect either (a) she rarely attends the meetings because she claims to be too busy (and her boss supports her choice to not attend) or (b) she attends but usually focuses on her phone and text messages during the meeting and doesn't participate very much; there is very little cross-business function information transfer from her to the others.

If you reset your expectation to the words and actions your bully will typically choose, you will not be surprised when it happens.

Learn to Laugh at the Bully's Behavior

Laughter can be helpful medicine for what ails you. Rehashing what happened with a workplace bully can strike your funny bone in a good way. Studies about laughter and its health benefits abound, but I'll give you some highlights here.

The Mayo Clinic reported on several studies that have shown the short term effects of laughter can include lowering your stress levels by changing your heart rate and blood pressure, thereby making you feel more relaxed. Laughter can also get your blood circulation moving and help your muscles to relax, which also lowers your feeling of stress.

In the long term, the Mayo Clinic also reports keeping laughter as a part of your regular routine will help to change negative thoughts and emotions to positive ones. Those negative thoughts and emotions we have can initiate chemical reactions in our cells that lower our immune system. By bringing laughter into our lives daily, we can stem the tide of negative thoughts and feelings and, by doing so, boost our immune system, as positive thoughts and feelings have been shown to release neuropeptides, which can lower our stress and keep our cells clean. Laughter has also been found to help release a natural pain killer and lower depression and anxiety.[8]

You can always watch a funny TV show, movie, or comedian to get you laughing. Or talk with your funniest friends who make you laugh.

This is usually helpful: Find a few friends who will let you tell your workplace bully stories. If it helps, pretend you're an actor on a sitcom and reenact the parts and the scene. You can speak their voice realistically or, like many comedians do when they mimic people, exaggerate it a bit. Act out the same gestures your workplace bully does.

If you want to make sure no one faults you for laughing at your own stories about your own bully, tell it to friends who don't work at your company.

Don't Blame Yourself

In many stories I've heard and read over several years about people who found themselves in abusive situations, it was common to hear that the victims often blamed themselves for the way their abuser treated them. Abusers are devious in the way that they can get their victims to think *they* are to blame for being treated abusively.

Even though I don't call subtle workplace bullies "abusive" (but I do call full-on bully bosses abusive), there are plenty of people who blame themselves for the bad behavior they get from their workplace bully.

Do you ever do that? Do you blame yourself for the poor behavior you get from your workplace bully? If you do, it's time to put a stop to blaming yourself!

Picture yourself as a person who does *not* deserve to be treated in any of the ways you've been treated by the workplace bully. Instead, think through how you prefer to be treated. Then tell yourself you deserve to be treated well.

Realize that your workplace bully *chooses* his behavior. He may allow other people to get on his nerves (for whatever reason), but even if you remind him of someone else who bothers him, he has a responsibility to treat you respectfully.

So stop blaming yourself for your workplace bully's choices!

If you find it's difficult to stop blaming yourself for how the workplace bully treats you, you may consider getting professional help from a counselor. Self-blame in this situation is a codependent behavior where you're enabling the workplace bully to continue being a bully (and you think his behavior is somehow your fault). A counselor can help you work through it so that you're no longer blaming yourself and no longer enabling the workplace bully.

If you are part of a faith community, you might also consider speaking with your faith's leader (pastor, priest, rabbi, etc.) for resources, such as a referral to a counselor or support group that can help you overcome enabling others or blaming yourself.

Don't Make Excuses for the Bully's Behavior

Some gentle people I've known have been likely to make excuses for people who've treated them badly, whether that person was a spouse, boyfriend or girlfriend, parent, sibling, child, or colleague.

Below are some excuses I've heard for workplace bullies and their behavior:

- That's just how he is. (Head shake here.)
- She brings good money into the company.
- He keeps our company competitive.
- I don't think she's done anything illegal.
- He's just joking around.
- Why would anyone feel bullied by her?
- We want our managers to be tough.
- He's going through a rough spot.

Can we just stop the madness?

If you fall into this category of making excuses for the workplace bully's behavior, please put some of your focus on not making excuses for this person's consistently bad behavior.

Don't minimize their behavior or its effect on you. Don't rationalize or intellectualize it. Call it what it is.

Excusing their behavior just enables them to continue bullying you and enables them to choose new targets in the future.

View Your Bully Situation as Temporary

Whenever we're in a life situation for which we can't circle a date on the calendar and say, "*This* is when 'abc' will be over," we need to work at resetting our thoughts about the permanence of the situation. That's not easy (especially when we're not actively pursuing a change). It takes some brain power and control over our will to internalize the fact that few situations are permanent.

When we can't see the "change date" on the calendar, we need to imagine that a "change date" exists anyhow. Imagine a change in your mind, consider what life will be like when that change occurs and you're free of the bullying behavior, let hope for the future settle inside you, and then bask in that feeling for a while. By then, envisioning your current situation as a *temporary situation* should be a lot easier, and your emotional response to even thinking about the workplace bully should have changed for the better.

It's difficult to be optimistic when you're the target of a workplace bully. However, it's by choosing to think about your situation differently that you can view your situation as temporary.

M.J. Ryan, a change specialist, cites research on resilience as finding that people who view a difficulty or setback as a temporary situation have a better chance of getting through it than people who are more pessimistic and cannot get their mind to stop thinking that the current situation won't change.[9]

Reframing your situation in your mind as *temporary* will help you to cope in a healthier manner.

Silence the Negative Critical Voice Inside of You

We all have an inner critic, but some people's inner critics are cruel while others are kind. If your inner critic is cruel, you will need to learn to shut it down. A cruel internal negative voice will usually occur in people who had a bully for a parent, grandparent, sibling, or teacher. Having a workplace bully in your life will only exacerbate the problem.

Rather than allow thoughts to fester in your mind as if there is a bully in your head telling you negative messages about yourself:

- Focus your time and mindset on brainstorming ideas to solve problems and then getting support for your ideas and solutions.
- Think of a few things you did well yesterday and last week (even seemingly small things).
- Spend more time on a favorite hobby or sport.
- Who gives you positive feedback? A friend or family member? People at a place where you volunteer? Spend some time with them or talk by phone.

Don't Play Their Games

Oh, the games people play, every night and every day! Both inside and outside the workplace, I've been confronted with a character I call "the drama queen." Usually a woman (but sometimes a man), she's a sub-type of workplace bully. I do not get along with drama queens!

Just like cats often seek out people who don't like cats, drama queens often seek out people who don't like to be around drama queens. They are conniving game-players who reserve their behavior for a few people. I'm getting shivers just thinking about them.

Drama queens will try to play a game with you. Years ago, I often played along, sometimes unknowingly. Then I got wise and refused to play their games. When I chose to not play their games, that often meant that I changed the game in some manner. Not playing their games or changing the game can lead to them getting angry, but that's okay. In their games, you always lose. If you refuse to play or change the game, you also change the outcome; instead, it will either come out even or you will win.

One of my most dramatic drama queens worked with me in a volunteer organization. She subtly worked toward undermining my work for the group. Her husband and I were among the leaders of the organization and she worked on him to the point where he wouldn't look me in the eye. She tried to set up situations so that she would be involved in whatever I was working on, and then she could more easily undermine my efforts.

For example, as a board member and treasurer, I set up all of the accounting policies and procedures. She worked in the office part time and often refused to follow the established procedures, such as reimbursing herself for expenses without submitting an expense report and receipts.

Another time, I oversaw an annual picnic and all of the details, such as reserving the outdoor space, organizing the details of the event, and managing the marketing. On the day of the picnic, she organized several games and even brought things with her to run the games. While the games were fun, she never discussed with me in advance her idea of organizing and leading games. She just did it, undermining and ignoring my leadership.

The head of the organization didn't want to deal with her drama and wouldn't confront her to put an end to it. Her constant, and often quiet, methods for drawing attention to herself, undermining me, and competing with me went unrecognized by most people.

In order to stop being a player in her games, I would figure out in advance what I could work on that she couldn't touch. I would find out what she was working on and steer clear. She also had a habit of volunteering to do something only to drop the ball so that someone else would have to clean it up. I made certain that when she chose to drop the ball she would have to clean it up.

Do you see what I'm saying? I changed the game she set up. She created games to undermine my work, and I changed the game so that she couldn't undermine me. She also created games so that she could drop the ball and make messes that other people would have to clean up. I changed that game so that she would have to clean up her own messes.

If she wasn't a drama queen, there wouldn't have been a game in the first place. She set up a game with her own rules that I couldn't win. You could call it her "zero sum game." I figured it out. Then I changed the game.

She was mad. Too bad!

Drama queens from my past have wanted me to be on their spinning merry-go-'rounds until I got nauseous! Because I wouldn't play their games, they would find ways to "punish" me. This could include talking badly about me to others, doing work behind my back, or any of a number of bullying behaviors you've already read about in this book.

It really is unbelievable to remember those situations now, looking at them from 10,000 feet away and seeing how ridiculous their behavior really was. But when I was in the midst of it, being so mistreated because I wouldn't play along, I felt a lot of stress in my life because of these dramatic people.

Not all workplace bullies are drama queens, but all drama queens are bullies in some manner.

Workplace bullies often will choose to play games with you. If you choose to not play along they will probably get angry. For some of you, the stress of bearing their anger is more than the stress you'd experience from just playing along with their game. But at what cost?

So I want you to think about what can happen if, next time, you choose to *not* play their game. What are all of the possibilities? What are the worst-case scenarios? What are the best-case scenarios? Or, instead of not playing their game at all, can you change the game so that you don't lose?

Then, after brainstorming all of the possible outcomes, for each one, consider: *So what if that happened?*

Here is an example of dealing with a drama queen/workplace bully in this fashion:

Situation:	The workplace bully sends you emails over and over with ridiculous questions every time you send out an email to a particular group of people. It feels like the same old game every time. She wants you to get on her merry-go-'round again. Or, you feel like you're a puppet and she has commanded you to "dance"! You've had enough and you want the game to stop.
What are the possibilities?	Don't reply to her emails any longer. Just ignore them. (This means you're choosing to not play her game.)
Best Case Scenario	She stops sending these emails. (She stops playing her game.)

Worst Case Scenarios	A. She emails even more frequently and/or annoyingly.
	B. She goes to your boss to complain that you haven't replied to her emails.
	C. She is your boss. She complains to you that you haven't replied to her emails.
So, what if that happened?	A. Go back to all of her emails of this type. Save the emails to a flash drive. This is easy to do in Outlook. If you have another email system, find another way to save her emails, even if you have to copy & paste them into Word. The sheer number of these, when read back-to-back, will show her up as a drama queen. Keep the emails on your flash drive. You never know when they will come in handy. Just continue to ignore her emails.
	B. Save all of her emails, just as in "A" above. Take these to your boss. Reveal the craziness of it all. Get your boss on your side. If your boss won't see it your way, see Option 3 in this chapter.
	C. Save all of her emails, as in "A" above. See Option 3 in this chapter. It's time to find a new job.

Lastly, go through each of the previous points regarding pulling away emotionally. Reset your expectations for the behavior of your workplace bully. Don't blame yourself for his choices. See your situation as being temporary. And work toward "not caring" about how he responds.

Find Others Who Understand

There is strength in numbers, and while it's easier to find people who "get it" when your boss is a bully, certainly over time *someone* will also experience the bullying ways of your workplace bully. Even if you find just one other person at work to listen, talking about it with someone who understands firsthand what it is like to be on the workplace bully's receiving end can be a stress reliever and help you cope with your situation.

Another stress-reducer is telling your story to friends and family. Even when you tell your story outside the workplace to them, however, keep your story as fact-based as possible, leaving out the emotion and drama.

Getting a few family members and friends to be supportive of you as you journey through the workplace bully situation is critical. Hopefully, you can count on several of them to be your listeners and cheerleaders.

If any of your family members or friends tell you, "Just let it go," or something of that nature, they may not understand anything about what bullying does to people. If the people who say things such as, "Just let it go," to you don't want to learn and change in order to support you in this process, then you will need to find a few other people who *do* want to learn how to actively support you and then follow through and actually do it.

What if My Bully is a Narcissist?

In a previous chapter, we defined a narcissist and determined that while many workplace bullies are not narcissists, all narcissists in the workplace will become a bully.

If you've identified your workplace bully as a narcissist, there are a few things you can do while you're working with them to ease the pain.

First, tell them how you feel—about anything. Tell them how you feel about a project, a decision, being told you can't take time off—anything that is either a small deal or a big deal to you. Then see how he responds. Talking about emotions is a problem for narcissists. He might squirm. If you can stand watching him squirm, go ahead and give this a try.

Another idea regards discussions that involve problems and solutions. Get the conversation to focus on brainstorming solutions and then narrow down the list to choosing one solution. Narcissists prefer to get stuck on a problem and take the problem apart bit by bit. They don't want to get to the solution. Guide the conversation to the resolution as quickly as you can. Start with a variety of solution ideas—this is where brainstorming several ideas to solve the problem is helpful. If he won't choose a solution and it's driving you crazy, leave him with the solution options and leave the meeting or phone call.

If your workplace bully/narcissist isn't all that bad of a bully, and you need for him to do something in particular, go ahead and shower him with a bit of admiration. Just grit your teeth and do it. He'll perform for you like a puppet for the positive attention.

A Few Other Tips

Be Selective About What You Believe

Even if the statements bullies make to you contain bits of truth, don't believe or accept what they say. Accepting a bully's message to you that contains lies, plus a bit of truth, will be damaging to you.

Let's say your bully tells you that you got some facts wrong in an email you sent but the way in which he communicates this to you suggests you are incompetent. The truth in this scenario is that you got some facts wrong. The lie is that you're incompetent. Don't believe the lie.

Set Your Goals Yourself

Don't let a bully "help" you set your goals at work. Even if the bully is your boss, set your own goals.

A bully doesn't have your best interests at heart. He may set goals for you that are unattainable, thus setting you up for failure.

Create your own goals. If you're in the early part of your career and not sure how to do it, ask a trusted colleague or someone outside your company to help you.

Constructive Anger is OK

People who are bullied in the workplace, who were also bullied when they were children (especially by a bully who acted angry), can have difficulty *now* with how angry they feel about the bullying. It's so important that they acknowledge they feel angry and then find constructive (instead of destructive) ways to deal with that anger.

Examples of destructive ways to handle anger:

- Lashing out at others
- Sweeping your feelings under a rug
- Using passive aggressive behaviors

Examples of constructive ways to handle anger:

- Using assertive methods to have conversations
- Working toward solving interpersonal problems in an assertive manner
- Retaining the dignity of everyone involved

When the Bully Plays the "Shame Card"

Many targets will feel shame after being bullied. Many bullies purposely play "the shame card" on their targets by trying to get their target to feel shameful about something.

I have seen this happen many times where bullies try to shame their targets. Interestingly, this doesn't work on me. When workplace bullies have tried this with me, I nearly burst out laughing either in their presence or later. Actually, later I do burst out laughing.

I don't intend to take lightly those of you who feel a sense of shame when the bully pulls a hat over your eyes. It is as if they want to close your eyes to the truth so that you feel badly about yourself.

Undoing the feeling of shame when you haven't done anything wrong (but they have) is one other thing you will need to focus on correcting so that undue shame doesn't take you down.

Shouldn't Human Resources Help Me?

I believe Human Resources (HR) representatives should always be willing and able to help people who have a workplace bully to deal with at the office, whether that bully is of the "lite" variety or not. But the truth is many human resource professionals are either not willing or not able to help (or both). I've also met some HR representatives who were willing to help a little, but only to a certain point.

In addition, I've heard stories of people speaking to an HR representative about a bully, and then the HR rep told the bully, "Your employee, John, is saying bad things about you." That's some bad HR!

If you take your story to HR, just be prepared for a response from them that you don't want to hear. This can include ignoring you, telling you the problem is you, or listening well but then not helping after all.

What HR Might Say or Do That Isn't Helpful

You would think that an HR representative would be best equipped to help you. That should be true, but sometimes it isn't. They might be afraid of the workplace bully.

Even if you get some help and good advice from an HR representative, you might later get poor advice when you go back to them and want them to be a sounding board.

If HR (or anyone for that matter) gives you advice *that comes from a place of fear*, don't go back to that HR representative.

When you're dealing with a bully-lite workplace bully, the worst thing you can do is go to a place of fear.

When you go to a place of fear, you embolden your workplace bully to be even more of a bully. Bullies want you to fear them! Do whatever you have to do to stop inviting fear of the workplace bully into your life. In order to do this, you will need to *stop listening* to anyone who adds fear to your situation. For anyone who goes to a place of fear and gives you "advice" that increases fear, stop telling them what is going on in your life. They will give you unsolicited advice based in fear. If HR does this, stop going to them.

I once spoke to an HR representative about a workplace bullying situation. She said, "When I'm in a situation like that, I grin and bear it."

I said, "What? That's terrible. I would never suggest someone 'grin and bear it' with a workplace bully."

She said, "Wait! Let me finish! I grin and bear it. But then …I'll get them back!"

I said, "You'll get revenge? Revenge is never a good idea."

She said, "But I'd do it in a nice way."

People, this is *not* good advice from HR!

What About Contacting the Employee Assistance Counselor?

At some companies, their benefits package includes access to an Employee Assistance Program (EAP), which allows employees to call an Employee Assistance counselor to discuss problems of any kind.

This sounds good on the surface. However, some research shows that occasionally EAP counselors are on management's side. These counselors often *don't* keep your conversation with them confidential. Their loyalty is to their customer (your employer!) who pays their bill. This is especially true if the EAP counselor is in-house and not a third party contractor.

If the EAP counselors are true counselors outside your company, they have a professional obligation to keep your conversation confidential. In addition, in the U.S., HIPAA rules prevent them from sharing what you tell them.

Before you contact the EAP, ask around at your company if anyone has heard whether other employees have had a good experience with them. If not, why not? Are they more loyal to the employer than they are to the employees?

Ethics & Compliance Office at Large Companies

Large companies often have an office of Ethics and Compliance. They will usually be the keepers of the company's "code of conduct." Check to see if your company has such a group or office. Typically they are made up of corporate attorneys. If your company has such an ethics group, ask to see the code of conduct. Get to know the people who belong to that group. Do they care that workplace bullying is going on? What about subtle bullying? If it's not illegal, do they care? Will they help you?

Consider Whether to Provide "Version 2" of Your Notes to HR

If you know what you want HR to do for you, write it out, bring it to your meeting, and review it with them. At least you can say you were clear about what you wanted when you spoke to them.

Earlier in this chapter, you read about *documenting everything.* Think about whether this is a good time to give HR "version 2" of your notes (or part of "version 2" of your notes). If not, then wait.

Bullying Could Be Systemic at a Company

Much of what I'm suggesting here—where HR will not help you—is indicative of a general leadership problem at most companies. While discussing this topic with several great corporate leaders I know (and have personally experienced working with over time), all of them had knowledge of, and may have witnessed, a corporate culture in HR that didn't care whether bullies were present at their company. In some cases, bullies actually worked in the HR department.

Some people in leadership are the bullies. A few of these bullies are quite dysfunctional and toxic. Most bullies in leadership are of the "lite" variety. A Bell curve of leadership probably looks like this:

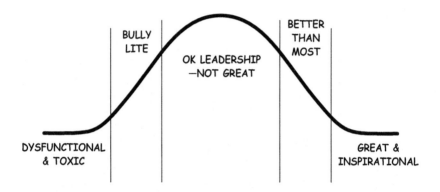

The title of this section is, "Shouldn't Human Resources Help Me?" The answer to that question is *yes*, but the really difficult and more important question is, "*Will* Human Resources help me?" The bottom line regarding HR is that they rarely will help the target of a workplace bully. Some will remain neutral. And some will make your situation worse for you.

Take Care of Yourself

Engaging in self-care during stressful times in life is important to your overall health and well-being. Doing so while being bullied at work is crucial.

It's critical that you take care of yourself mentally, emotionally, and physically. So far you've read enough about the workplace bully and his or her effect on you in order to (1) understand what has been happening to you and (2) define it accurately. You've also read about some coping strategies in Option 1 that will go a long way to take care of the mental and emotional stress. I have a few more ideas for you that hit the physical side of health (and some touch on the *physical* plus mental/emotional aspects):

- Get exercise
  - If you're busy, rather than join an exercise class that ties you to a schedule, join a gym that has long open hours.
  - Do some aerobic exercise: jogging, walking, race walking, elliptical machine, biking, swimming, etc.
  - Weight lifting
  - Gardening; housework (this only works as a stress reliever if you have the time for it)
  - Hire people to do household work for you. (I did this for gardening and housework, which was a huge stress reliever for me!)

- Schedule down-time.
  - High stress situations need more "down time," not less.
  - During down time: No computer, no stressful discussions, no stressful reading material.

- Sleep!
  - Most targets of bullying have trouble sleeping well. Do what you need to do in order to fit in more sleep.

- Find a good massage therapist.
  - Decide how often you can afford a massage. Or find someone who does chair massage which is a little less expensive.

A Warning

I mentioned at the beginning of this section that *choosing to cope without making any other changes* is not my favorite solution to the workplace bully problem. That is because, if you take too much garbage from the workplace bully over time, it may send him the wrong message. He may believe explicitly that you think his behavior is fine, you have no problem with it, and, therefore, why should *anyone* have a problem with him?

Let's look at Option 2.

Option 2: Stay at Your Job and Work Toward Getting the Bully to Change

If you choose to stay at the company in the same job and do more than simply cope, you've got to take action toward getting the workplace bully to change. Many of the coping strategies mentioned in the previous section will actually be very helpful for you as you wait for change to occur, so make sure you read that section ("Option 1") and decide what you want to do in order to make your work situation more livable in the meantime.

Trying to get a bully to change can be a huge task. For some types of bullies, many of us targets won't try because the stress factor is too high. In this section, I cover what needs to be in place for you to safely consider confronting the bully and how to get the bully to change.

Something that is necessary for the bully's bullying to be successful is that their target must experience self-doubt. You'll know that self-doubt has reared its ugly head inside of you when you get thoughts such as:

- Is something wrong with me?
- Something must be wrong with me.
- He is so confident in what he's saying, and I'm not feeling confident, so what he says must be true.
- I don't know if I should do or say anything about this. I don't want to make waves.

You will need to work on changing your self-doubt to self-confidence in what you know to be true before you confront the bully.

By the way, it is okay to feel angry about what the bully has done and how she has treated you. Funnel that anger in a constructive way, however, not in a destructive way. For example, taking revenge is destructive. Confronting is constructive.

When should you confront a workplace bully about his behavior? If you're going to do more than cope (Option 1), then you should confront shortly after you decide that confronting the bully is your best choice. Most of us wait too long to either confront or to find a new job, lengthening the time that we are recipients of their awful workplace bully behavior.

Many of you realize you *need a job* (this job for now) and you're reluctant to say anything about the bullying or take action to stop it.

Perhaps you feel you don't have a choice in the matter—you believe you *must* stay at the company and work through it; and your determination to do just that also fires up your desire to see change in the workplace bully.

If you're going to stay at your present company along with the workplace bully, this strategy is your best bet for getting back your sense of being in control of your workplace situation.

Confronting the workplace bully can restore your dignity and self-esteem.

Before I make this sound too easy, I'll tell you it's a lot of work to get changed behavior from the workplace bully. It takes persistence on your part to keep at it. How long can it take to see positive change? As long as a year or two. So you need to ask yourself, "Can I live with that timeframe? Or am I 'past that point' right now, and I need to see change in two months?—or else I need to leave!"

In 2012, the Workplace Bullying Institute (WBI) took a survey of 554 targets of workplace bullies to ask them about confronting the bully. Of those, 69% had confronted their bully and 31% did not confront at all.

Of the people who confronted their bully, only 6.5% got their bully to stop bullying them. Of those, 2% confronted immediately—right after the first incident, 2% confronted in the first few weeks after the first incident, and 2.5% confronted months after the first incident.

That is all who got the bully to change—6.5% of the people who chose to confront!

Of the remaining people who confronted their bully, 23% confronted immediately, 31.5% confronted in the first few weeks after the first incident, and 39% confronted months after the first incident.[10]

Please, choose Option 2, working to get the bully to change, after plenty of consideration.

In your mind, you might entertain the thought that the situation could get worse if the result of confronting the bully is some sort of retaliation against you. But if you don't confront it, the bullying won't stop. When you leave the company, the bully will find a new target if you don't become assertive and work to get the bullying to end.

Getting changed behavior from the workplace bully often starts with meeting with him. You can also set up situations and conversations so that your workplace bully feels the pain of his actions. In addition, one of the best ways to get lasting change out of your workplace bully is to use the help of an advocate.

Let's start by getting into the workplace bully's mind.

What is Going On Inside the Mind of a Bully?

Unlike non-bullies who respect people who are different from themselves as much as they respect people who are like them, bullies tend to only respect people who are similar to them. That means they mainly respect people who will counter them with aggression right back.

Workplace bullies often try out their bullying behavior on several people to see who pushes back and who doesn't. Those who don't become a target.

For some of you, pushing back just isn't in your nature. The thought of doing so raises a red flag for you, increases fear inside you, or may even repulse you.

For others of you, your faith tradition/religion tells you that you should "turn the other cheek" to the workplace bully. Or it tells you that you shouldn't respond to the workplace bully by being aggressive or assertive. It's more of a response of "no action." However, a bully interprets turning the other cheek as *weakness*. He sees it as your submission to him and then you continue to be a target.

In the Bible alone, many stories are told where people stood up to authority figures and bullies of all kinds. In other faith traditions/religions you will find stories and examples of people asserting themselves toward bullies.

I believe there is a response to the bully that is neither giving him the same aggressive treatment *nor* inaction. Rather, it's an assertive response that he cannot misinterpret as submission. If you're like me, however, by the time I figure out how to respond in an assertive manner (not lashing out, not bullying back, not keeping quiet, not being submissive), it's three days later! Still, three days is not too late to go back to the bully to be assertive.

Bullies are usually competitive people and want to surround themselves with compliant people (especially the people who report to them). Other words to describe the people bullies prefer are cooperative, helpful, and accommodating. Compliant people are *not* those people the bullies respect. Remember, they respect people who will stand up to them.

Who have *you* been to the workplace bully so far? If we could get inside the bully's mind, what would we see when she thinks about you? Would we see:

- Someone she respects?
- Someone who stands up to her?
- A person she sees as a wimp?
- Someone who is easily manipulated?
- An employee who doesn't confront bad behavior in others?
- A person who is easy to control?
- Someone who is compliant? Never assertive and never aggressive?

This is a tough way to look at yourself. However, in order to get into the workplace bully's mind and see how it works and what it responds well to, we need to see how the workplace bully views you.

I want you to know the truth and get riled up a bit in order to take action!

Enlist the Help of an Advocate

Does your workplace bully respect (and even fear) someone at the office? Could that person be your advocate? This is probably the best alternative for getting the person to change his or her bullying behavior and for reducing the amount of your stress.

An advocate (or "sponsor") is someone who will go to bat for you—in this case, deal with your workplace bully to get him to change some of his bullying ways. The advocate will talk to the workplace bully, tell him how to treat you, hold him accountable for his behavior, and perhaps stir up some fear inside him for not cooperating.

This is what I've done a couple times and it has worked well. It's helpful to try to talk with the workplace bully yourself first, before going to the advocate. It is also helpful if you, the workplace bully, and the advocate can meet together. If that is not possible, a discussion between the two of them while you are absent is the next best thing.

In the example I'm recalling, my advocate was a former boss of my workplace bully, but not a current boss. They were on the same committee for a project I worked on. My advocate also said later, regarding my workplace bully, that "he responds well to fear" (meaning the advocate set up the communications between them so that the workplace bully would feel fear and that he would change his behavior positively because of that fear). It may have been fear or the workplace bully may have respected the advocate's position in the company enough to care about what the advocate said and what he requested in regard to me.

The advocate needs to know and understand the workplace bully from experience and needs to understand the issues at hand. However, the advocate does *not* need to be the workplace bully's boss.

Most bosses of bullies like (and even love) their bully/employee and don't see the bully as a bully. Before you speak to your bully's boss, find out if he loves the bully and views him through rose colored glasses. If so, don't speak to that boss. It will only bring you more pain.

Identify Potential Advocates

If this is a step you'd like to pursue, start by brainstorming potential advocates at your company. Make a list of people whose titles are higher than the bully's. Unless you can find a strong, supportive HR person, skip people who are in HR. If you perceive the bully's boss won't be supportive of you, skip him, too. Add people your bully respects to the list.

Next, go through each person on your list and note what you believe are the pros and cons of asking that person to be an advocate for you. Are any of the people on your list already aware of the bully's tendency to mistreat others? If so, do they think the bully's mistreatment of other employees is unprofessional, detrimental, and/or harmful to individual employees or to the company? Put a star by their names.

In the meantime, make certain your documentation of incidences is current, as described earlier. The advocate might want to know about specific examples of bullying behavior.

Choose an Advocate

Select your number one choice for an advocate. Request an appointment. During the meeting, give him a brief summary of what has been happening. Tell him you're looking for an advocate to go to bat for you, and you're wondering if he would consider filling that role.

He might ask what you envision his role as your advocate to be. Even if he doesn't ask, discuss what you're asking him to do.

You want him to help you deal with the workplace bully to get the bully to change his behavior. You want the advocate to meet with the bully, tell the bully how to treat you, hold the bully accountable for his behavior, and get the bully to feel fear if he doesn't cooperate.

The advocate can meet with your workplace bully either with or without you. This is a process, not a one-time event or single meeting with the advocate.

Whenever you update the advocate, be brief and to the point, giving an executive overview of the problem. If the advocate and workplace bully talk together in your absence, get an update from the advocate after the meeting, noting the points discussed, the position taken by the advocate during their meeting, agreements made, and the advocate's perceived response by the workplace bully.

Then schedule a new meeting with the workplace bully, making certain you are not upset when you meet. If possible, schedule a meeting for a few days later.

Keep your advocate informed of the progress made in the workplace bully's behavior, even if you see no change. The advocate may need to speak with the workplace bully more than once.

The advocate will often be *the key* to a successful change in the workplace bully that allows you to continue working at the company without the awful stress that has accompanied working with the workplace bully thus far.

Meet with the Workplace Bully

Meeting with the workplace bully is an important step. It's not pleasant. But as long as the workplace bully is not a "toxic" or abusive person (as you read about earlier) but is more of a bully-lite, you probably won't be verbally attacked, although you will probably get pushback.

Assuming you get a chance to meet with him, I have some ideas to get you ready for the meeting.

The first is about gaining confidence before you meet with the bully. There are some interesting socio-psychological studies that were done by social psychologist Amy Cuddy about body language and confidence. Her studies found that when a person who doesn't feel confident purposely practices putting their body into confidence-building stances, their internal confidence increases, and other people perceive them as being confident. Because of this, the person who didn't really feel confident and then did the confidence-building postures usually got what they asked for from the other person. Amy Cuddy calls it "fake it until you become it."

Do an Internet search on "Amy Cuddy" to see brief videos of her discussing her findings along with demonstrations of the physical stances people practiced before a meeting and the postures they assumed while in a meeting. She also shows stances and postures to avoid. She suggests practicing in a private conference room or a bathroom stall before a meeting. Try this several days before meeting with the bully to see if it helps increase your confidence.

When you finally meet with the bully, because some WBs tend to talk very fast and to think while you are talking (rather than listen to you), remember to speak slowly. When you take a turn to talk, count one or two seconds before you start. Be deliberate. If necessary, write out notes beforehand, bring the notes with you to the meeting, and use them. Notes will help you stay focused.

Start the conversation by mentioning something positive. For example, "When I first heard that you were selected to manage the project, I was glad about that because I knew you were bringing a lot of experience to the project."

Something like that.

Then begin to get to your point.

- Don't back down on the issues or wimp out.
- Don't make excuses for the workplace bully.
- Don't accept his or her excuses (you can listen without agreeing).

See where the conversation goes as you discuss your points.

- Are you getting any agreement?
- Is there evidence that you are being manipulated?
- Is the workplace bully displaying dysfunctional behaviors?
- Is the workplace bully trying to fight with you or is she trying to solve problems?
- Earlier in the book you read about agreeing to disagree *agreeably*. Can the workplace bully agree to disagree with you *agreeably*? In other words, are you sensing that the remaining disagreement between you and the workplace bully isn't also resulting in you feeling badly about it? Do you feel good about how the conversation

went, even if there are points the two of you still disagree about? Or does he agree to disagree *in a disagreeable fashion?* Is a remaining disagreement also leading you to feel badly? Has he cut you down in some way for the points you disagree about?

This ability of the other person to disagree with you *agreeably* is important if you are ever going to get to the point where working with the workplace bully on a daily basis is do-able and more-than-a-little-tolerable. (This is actually important for all relationships.)

It's important that you don't tell the workplace bully about any earlier negative experiences you've had with another bully at a prior workplace, school, or in your family. Also, don't tell him about prior traumatic experiences, depression, or any other negative trial. *It is none of his business.*

Make the Workplace Bully "Feel the Pain"

Any time you can get your workplace bully to feel the pain surrounding his poor management abilities, you've got an easy win! There is a skill to doing this and you can learn it. Some of it is by trial and error, and after a few tries, you'll see him squirming, changing his policies to what they should have been in the first place, and maybe even treating you more nicely. Ah, victory!

Thinking back to one of my WBs, Jerry, I wanted him to *feel the pain* of his decision to have us reconcile items that could not really be reconciled. (He wanted to see a one-for-one relationship between items for which there was not always a one-for-one ratio.) He had been badgering me about this for two weeks.

My goal was to motivate Jerry to make a different decision than he had originally made. He asked a group of us to complete an impossible task; I wanted him to change the task to something more reasonable and do-able.

To get to that goal, I needed to get Jerry to the point of *feeling the pain* of his original decision. This was no small task.

I spoke slowly to walk him through one of the "impossible tasks" that he created for people to perform. I answered his questions along the way, which included:

"Why can't this be done?"

And then I would explain why.

"But you have to have one entry from Schedule A fit into one entry on Schedule B," he'd say.

And I responded that it doesn't work that way because (and I explained with a bit of detail).

We kept going back and forth like this for almost a minute. Finally he put his head in his hands, and I knew *we hit pain!*

Ah, pain. If only all workplace bullies could feel the pain. At that painful point, he made a new decision. He told me that the way I had performed the evaluation was fine and I was done with the "impossible task."

There were two other people in the room at this meeting, so there were witnesses present. Would he have felt the pain in that short amount of time if there had not been two additional people in the room? I don't know. Months earlier, when he was even more jerky, I definitely would have needed the other people in the room in order for him to be patient enough to allow me to ask questions, receive answers, feel the pain, and change his direction for the task. By the time this incident occurred, he had mellowed a bit, so I might have had the same result if no one else was at the meeting.

But why take that chance? When you need for your workplace bully to feel pain, he might respond better with other people in the room. *Witnesses are a good thing.*

Look for very specific circumstances when you can get the workplace bully to feel pain about his own decisions. Write out your thoughts ahead of time regarding:

- What is going on?
- What did the workplace bully do?
- What do you believe he should have done (had he not been a workplace bully)?
- What truths does he need to understand?
- What are some ideas for getting that truth in front of him?
- What points do you need to make?
- What are the best ways you can communicate it in as brief an amount of time as possible?
- How can you get his attention?
- How can you "hammer home" your points?

Power and Powerlessness

A result of being bullied (besides the physical and emotional symptoms) is that the pain you feel can cause powerlessness. Feeling powerless can lead you to seek power.

I want to help you to *not* go to a dark place if the bullying makes you feel powerless. Do not try to increase your power. Gaining power is a trap, not a solution.

For example, if you respond to feelings of powerlessness by planning revenge, holding a grudge, staying bitter, retaliating through passive aggression, or going into rages, you are not going to get through this in a healthy manner.

While I've said that bullies respect strength and respect people who stand up to them, but do not respect people who submit to their bullying, I'm *not* advocating that you employ power actions to stop the bullying. Rather, I'm advocating for you to become assertive and to not submit to the bully's actions. Assertiveness and standing up to the bully *doesn't* involve power.

❖ Bully/Target Continuum-Triangle ❖

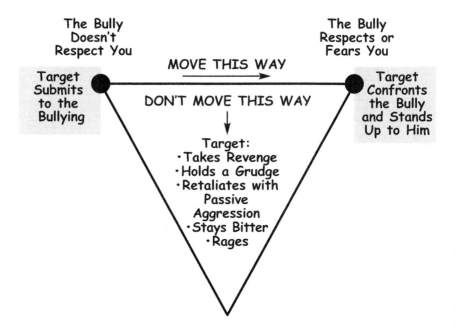

The Bully
Doesn't
Respect You

The Bully
Respects or
Fears You

MOVE THIS WAY

Target
Submits
to the
Bullying

DON'T MOVE THIS WAY

Target
Confronts
the Bully
and Stands
Up to Him

Target:
· Takes Revenge
· Holds a Grudge
· Retaliates with
  Passive
  Aggression
· Stays Bitter
· Rages

A Word about Workplace Bullying and Speaking the Truth

Being the target of a workplace bully causes damage. That damage can manifest itself emotionally and physically. Healing must occur in order for you to get better. For healing to take place, the truth must be told….*spoken out loud.*

People may tell you to keep the truth to yourself. Why do they say that? *Because they're afraid.*

Afraid of what?

They're afraid of the bully, afraid of conflict, afraid of what might happen, or afraid of the unknown.

A corporate leader told me he thinks most workplaces look like the following Bell curve:

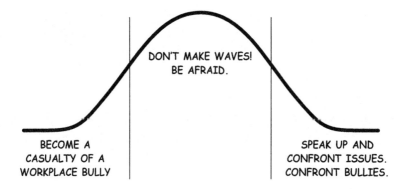

A few people become a casualty of a workplace bully. A few will speak up and confront issues, including confronting a bully. But most people are afraid to speak up on their own behalf or on others' behalf. They are afraid of what you read above.

Should you keep quiet?

No! Keeping quiet won't allow you to heal. The stress will eat you up if you don't tell your story and talk it out.

That doesn't mean you "shout it from the rooftops." It means smartly choosing people to whom you will tell your story:

- They will listen.
- They will be a sounding board.
- If they give advice, it is not fear-based. Rather, it is helpful.
- They might take on the role of an advocate.

Tell your story. Tell the truth. Healing comes from telling the truth.

More about HR: How to Know When They're Really Helping You

You might choose to speak to someone in Human Resources about your situation and experiences.

You will know an HR representative is helping you when you find out they took positive action after you spoke to them.

This might involve meetings or calls between the HR rep and your workplace bully's boss, conversations between the HR rep and the workplace bully, or both. If you see improved behavior in the workplace bully as a result of the HR rep's actions, you will know they helped you and made a positive difference.

It is also possible that after the HR rep has these conversations with the bully's boss or directly with the bully you don't see improved behavior or the bully becomes more of a bully. In this case, it's great that HR stepped in and made an attempt. At least you know they agreed with you even if their opinion wasn't respected. This is a clue you need to look for a new job, when an HR rep stands up for what is right, but their opinion is disrespected.

Remember this: HR actually represents the interests of the company. They *do not* represent you, the employee. If they choose to take action and stand up for you, that is a bonus. Most of the time (and from the stories I hear), HR does not stand up for, or advocate for, bullied employees.

And sometimes an HR rep is the bully!

Can *You* Be an Advocate in the Future?

Maybe while reading this you've thought of people who have mentioned bullying behavior from colleagues in their work life and they haven't been able to get the person to change. Now that you know about the importance of the role of an advocate, could you be an advocate for someone else at your company?

The advocate is an important role in a company in being a catalyst for change—making the workplace a better place to spend 40+ hours a week.

Please keep that in mind for the rest of your career. Former targets of WBs make great advocates for someone else!

A Story of a Workplace Bully Confronted that Leads to a Good Ending

In the last chapter, I mentioned a workplace bully at a client's office. I learned he had a reputation for not treating women well. He had subtly bullied one of my female colleagues and me. Then I found out he was telling people a lie about me.

I had used the help of an advocate earlier to get the workplace bully to stop mistreating my colleague and me. It was going fairly well. When I heard about the lie he was telling others about me, I did "damage control" by meeting with every upper level person I knew to clean up any potential mess.

One of the people I met with was an HR director. During the course of our conversation, I mentioned I had learned my workplace bully had a history of not treating women well. This HR rep (one of the fantastic HR reps, by the way) took the information and ran with it. She investigated it and wouldn't let it go until she was satisfied he would change his treatment of female colleagues. This was bold for the HR director to do since the bully's boss *loved him.*

Long story short—three years later I realized a woman from the company (with whom I was still friends) had to work with the workplace bully regularly. She was exactly the type of woman he would put down and belittle. By this time she had been working with him as a colleague for two years.

I asked her, "How does Nick treat you?"

She said, "Fine."

I said, "What? Really? He never gives you difficulty? He never puts you down or puts your ideas down?"

She said, "No. Never."

BAM! That is one of the times that a subtle workplace bully changed his ways after being confronted, first by me, then by the advocate, and later through the efforts of an HR director.

Option 3: Find a New Job

Your coping skills are on their last thread. Your workplace bully resists change. She keeps up the same old behaviors. Your stress level is consistently on the high side.

Sometimes, you just have to move on to a new job.

At a large company this can mean taking a new job in a different department and staying at your current company.

In fact, this is a best case scenario—if you work at a large organization, do they consider current employees for open positions? If you haven't done so, start networking inside the company to get acquainted with other people in departments that have no connection to the workplace bully.

If you work for a small company or if there aren't any other departments at your current large company that would mean you could get a different job there *and* be away from your workplace bully, then you will need to find a new job at a new organization.

Here's the deal: *Life is too short.* So when you spend a lot of time with someone who is a bully, it wastes precious time and energy. These people will suck you dry. Sometimes, it will just take too long to get your workplace bully to change and you are beyond the point of being patient. That is when *you know* you need to find another job.

When the cost of staying at a company is too high, it's time to move on. Update your résumé. Hopefully you have been networking with people on a regular basis. Now is the time to call on them for help finding a new job. Tell them about the type of position you're looking for and the skills you bring to the table.

Find career transition groups in your area that will help you brush up on your interviewing skills, networking skills, and will point you in other good directions.

If You Choose to Find a New Job

If you decide it's time to move on, keep in mind it might take a while to find a new job. In the meantime, read over Option 1 again. Learn the coping skills reviewed in that section and then put them into practice.

I've heard from many people who were once in a workplace bullying situation who quit their jobs without finding a new job first. They have told me if they had learned several coping strategies before choosing to quit it would have helped them temporarily preserve their dignity and income—while lowering their stress levels—as they looked for a new job.

———————

Those are your three options:

1. Stay at your current job, learn to cope with the bully, and do little to motivate the bully to change.
2. Stay at your current job and work toward getting the bully to change. Find an advocate to help you.
3. Find a new job. (This may take some time. Therefore, you will need to learn and practice coping skills so that the stress doesn't get the best of you in the meantime.)

As you read about each, which option stood out to you as most do-able?

———————

It would be best if you didn't take a job reporting to a workplace bully in the first place, right? In the next chapter, we'll look at how to identify a workplace bully during a job interview.

5

How to Identify a Workplace Bully During an Interview

"Not everyone has a right to his own opinion.
If he doesn't know the facts, his opinion doesn't count."

—Andy Rooney

Interviewing works both ways.

I've often told young adults that interviewing for a job is a lot like dating: people show you their best behavior during an interview. Therefore, if you see bad behavior during an interview, it's only going to get worse when you're working together. Of course, for young adults such as college students about to embark on their career, I'm talking about when they're the interviewee and the interviewer is their potential next boss.

Reflect back on all of the people you've dated. Think about the first three dates with each person (and the phone calls with him or her at that time). Whatever behavior you saw in (and heard from) those people during the first few dates represented their best behavior. Consider that for a moment. For most of them, any ways they might have acted or treated you that you would call "negative" typically didn't appear that early; rather, it showed up later (if at all). However, some of those people might have shown negative behavior on the first three dates. My point is this: Those people you dated showed you *their best self* in the first three dates. If you saw any hint of bad behavior early-on, that was a warning.

Some of you are reading this and recalling people you dated who displayed some negative behaviors by the third date, and you stuck around, giving him or her the benefit of the doubt because "everyone has a bad day." But that was a date! If they were having such a bad day that it would possibly affect their behavior when going out with you, they should have cancelled the date. The point is, they probably weren't having a bad day. Your date showed you who they really are.

Others of you are remembering people you dated who showed these types of negative behaviors early-on and you ended the relationship right away, keeping it from ever going forward. You knew that people show their best behavior early in a relationship. So if this was their "best" behavior, you knew you did not want to stick around.

Going on job interviews is a lot like the early days of dating: If you see bad behavior at the interviewing stage, it's not going to get much better. Just like the fact that your date will not treat you any better than he or she does on the first few dates, the manager who is interviewing you is not going to treat you any better once you take the job than the behavior you observe in him during the interview process. If you see rude behavior on those first few "dates" (interviews and phone calls), you're going to get even more rude behavior later!

Years ago, I interviewed for a job at a software company to do post-sales consulting. My original interview was with the operations manager. He seemed pretty normal. For my second interview, I met with someone who would be a co-worker. She seemed normal, too. Both interviews went well. I heard from the operations manager shortly thereafter, and he said I would receive a call from someone in the department who was his new assistant operations manager (I'll call him Matt). Matt called me a day later and gave me the job offer. I asked a few questions to clarify the full offer's package, thanked him, and told him I would think about the offer for a day or two and would get back to him.

Matt said, "You have to *think* about it?" (And then he included a sarcastic little chuckle.)

I thought, "What is his problem?"

However, I said, "Yes, and I'll call you back in a day or two."

That was my first warning sign of what was to come.

I took the job thinking I would report to the normal operations manager. However, I soon found out that the entire department now reported to Matt, not to the operations manager. Matt proved to be a true subtle workplace bully. He never yelled. He never berated someone at a meeting. He just had a coy, passive-aggressive, sarcastic way of putting me (and a few others) down.

Since Matt didn't actually interview me, I didn't have any experience with him during the interview process. Only through the initial job offer did I first speak to him, and that was a red flag. However, at the time I didn't understand that I would actually *report* to Matt. I thought I would report directly to the operations manager and that Matt would be inconsequential. This change to make Matt the boss occurred just as they were making the job offer to me. Therefore, I didn't actually have the opportunity to *experience* Matt until I accepted the job. Fortunately, this is the exception to the rule: Normally, you'll be interviewed by the person who will be your boss.

We all hope we'll be treated with respect and courtesy when we interview for a job. Besides looking out for rude workplace bully behavior during an interview, you also need to look out for "Dr. Jekyll." This is the person who acts kindly during the interview but who reveals his jerky "Mr. Hyde" ways after you take the job. He is able to appear normal and low maintenance in certain situations, but his bullying ways appear later.

So before you "marry" a job, it's important to know some things to look for during an interview with your future boss (and even with future co-workers). If you figure out how to identify a workplace bully during an interview, you will save yourself from many headaches later.

While I worked for Matt-the-workplace-bully, I went on an interview at another software firm. This time I interviewed with someone from HR and with the operations manager (who would be my boss). I'll call him John. This man seemed to have difficulty focusing on the matter at hand. At one point, I asked John a question and, rather than answer it, he went on to something else as if I had not asked the question at all.

I wondered, "Am I invisible?"

I left there knowing I did not want the job.

After I got back to the office, I saw a co-worker who liked to travel for business and it struck me that he might actually like the position and the company. I told him I had just been on an interview with XYZ Software firm, the position had a lot of travel, and that he might like to look into it.

He replied, "No, I don't want to work there. That would mean working for John, and he's a @#$%&!"

I said, "Oh, so you know John already." He shot me a knowing glance.

I thought, "My intuition is working well!"

How do you figure out during the interview if your future boss is a workplace bully? What do you look for? How do you use *your* intuition?

Here are some behaviors and tendencies you want to look for, listen for, and be aware of during the interview process:

- He doesn't look you in the eye often enough.
- She doesn't listen to your question or comment and her next statement following yours is unrelated to what you just said.
- It seems like he didn't listen to your question.
- She interrupts you.

- In his response to your question, he seems to dismiss your question or slightly put you down (rather than just answer your question).
- She is contrarian: You say "black," she says, "white." You say, "white," she says, "black."
- You sense his need to always be right by the words and phrases he chooses.
- He always has to have the last word or "corrects" you when you're speaking during the interview.
- At the end of the interview, you have the impression of her self-importance.
- He makes a comment inferring that you don't have the "right" to negotiate or to think about a job offer for a day.

Here are additional ideas to filter out a potential bad boss during the interview process:

- During your interview with your potential boss, ask:
  - How would you describe your management style?
  - How would your employees describe you?
  - How would your peers describe you?
    - Is he or she comfortable answering these questions?
    - Do you sense that he or she demeans their directly reporting employees or peers?
- Ask to interview with people who would be your coworkers. (They report to the same person who would be your boss.)
  - If you're wondering how to ask, wait until they are scheduling for your first in-person interview. Before the recruiter (or whoever you're speaking to) finishes the call, if she hasn't mentioned that you'll be interviewing with someone who would be a coworker, ask the recruiter if it would be possible for you to interview with someone who would be a coworker who reports to the hiring manager. She might say yes.

- On the day of the interview, have a list of questions ready, including questions about their thoughts regarding working at the company, working in the department, and weave in a question or two about working for the boss.
- When you ask questions about the boss, pay close attention to their eyes, facial expressions, and body language.
- If you're going to be in management or upper management, ask to interview with one or two peers of the boss.
  - Ask these people what the boss is like to work with.
  - Do they answer your questions directly?
  - Do you think they're being honest?
  - Do they seem uncomfortable answering your questions?
- When you interview with HR, about the potential boss ask them:
  - How would you describe his management style?
  - How have people who worked for him described him?

If you see hints of bad behavior during the interview process, run!

For an additional "check," do an Internet search on your boss. Some websites exist where people write their opinions about workplaces and bosses. You might be able to find out what other people (anonymously!) have to say.

Some people who read this book may be looking for ways to help someone who's being bullied at work. Or if you're being bullied, maybe you know someone who can help you—people who want to know what to do and what *not* to do.

In the next chapter, we review how to help someone who's being bullied.

6

How to Help Someone Else Who's Being Bullied

"If you are neutral in situations of injustice, you have chosen the side of the oppressor. If an elephant has its foot on the tail of a mouse, and you say that you are neutral, the mouse will not appreciate your neutrality."

—Desmond Tutu

Helping someone navigate the awful experience of workplace bullying can help them get to a better place faster. By "a better place," I mean when:

- They're no longer having the physical and emotional symptoms of being bullied,
- They've figured out ways to cope,
- Possibly they've figured out how they are going to confront the bully, and/or
- They have a plan for finding a new job.

This chapter is intended to give the targets of workplace bullying the opportunity to (1) identify how the people in their life can help them and then (2) give their friend or colleague a chapter to read that helps the friend or colleague understand what they can do to help the target.

I'm defining a *friend* of the target as someone who doesn't work at the same company. This includes family and it can include former coworkers. I'm defining a *colleague* of the target as someone who currently works at the same company.

Friends of targets can certainly help the target navigate the journey of ending the bullying. Colleagues of the target can help, too, depending on their position, work relationships, and connection to the bully.

The rest of this chapter is addressed to you, the friend or colleague of the target. The target you know may have already read this chapter and made notes or highlighted sections of importance to him or her.

I want you to understand what you can do to really help the target of a bully and I also want you to be aware of actions that might seem to be helpful on the surface but that are frustrating and create more stress for the target.

Some targets of workplace bullying might not have yet defined the actions of the bully *as bullying*. The behaviors of the bully might have been so subtle that calling it *bullying* would sound harsh to some people.

You can help the target of a subtle bully begin the process of calling the behavior bullying. Once the target acknowledges they're being bullied, you can help them with some of the process that leads to having no more symptoms, the end of the bullying, and/or the target finding a new job.

One of the most important things you can do to help someone who is being bullied at work is to *listen*.

Let's say this person you know hasn't quite come to the point of realizing the situation they're in at work is actually a form of bullying. He tells you a story about something that occurred at their workplace, and, to you, it sounds like a form of bullying.

First, ask him questions that will help him to verify (or even come to the point of admitting) that he is being bullied by a person at work. For example, you may ask:

Has anything like this happened with this person before? If so, what else happened?

Has this person ever exhibited behaviors in the past that caused you to feel stressed? If so, what happened then? How have you felt when this person treated you this way?

Based on the definitions of workplace bullying described earlier in this book (ok, I admit it—it would be helpful if you read the entire book!), ask if he feels targeted by this person for bad behavior. Help him to understand the definitions of workplace bullying, how the target of a bully will likely feel, and the usual symptoms of being bullied in the workplace, even if the bullying is subtle. Help him acknowledge the person at his workplace has targeted him for bullying.

I interviewed many targets of workplace bullying to find out, while the bullying was occurring:

- What other people did or said that *wasn't* helpful (and was possibly even hurtful).
- What other people did or said that was helpful, encouraging, and/or gave them ideas about how they might deal with the bullying.
- What people could have said or done that would have been helpful, encouraging, etc., but no one did.

The "Don'ts"

Let's start with the things people experienced from others that *wasn't* helpful.

Being bullied is difficult to talk about for many people. Listen to your friend or colleague without inundating them with your own thoughts and ideas.

- When she tells you what's happening, don't tell her, "You should do _____" or "You shouldn't do _____"
- Don't ask her "Have you tried doing this _____?"
- Don't interrupt her when she's talking.
- Rather than talk about *your* thoughts, ideas, and

feelings about her situation, listen to her and *validate her* experiences, thoughts, ideas, and opinions.

As you validate the target and what she tells you about her experiences, it will encourage her to talk more and to begin to pull her thoughts together.

Don't try to solve the problem for her (especially if you're a friend who doesn't work at the same company). As you listen and validate what she says, she will come up with some solutions on her own.

Some targets of workplace bullies are gentle souls who don't toot their own horn or talk about themselves very often. Don't scold someone who doesn't take credit for their successes. (The bullies already scold them—don't do that to them more!) Rather, say, "Oh, I think your own capabilities led to _____!" Help to build their self-confidence by helping them to see that their own skills, talents, and competence led to a success.

While targets tend to not take credit for their successes, they will take credit for failures. Help them turn that around.

If you work at the same company, don't discuss your colleague's bullying situation with other people (unless you are the Advocate and have the target's permission to do so).

After listening to the target, don't say:

I don't know what to say. I've never been in that situation before.

She's not asking if you've been in that situation before. She wants you to be a good listener, so that she can "think out loud," which will lead her to come to some conclusions and decisions on her own. Can you put yourself in her shoes for one hour and consider ideas about what she might do to cope, confront, and/or find a new job?

Don't be overly cheerful when the target tells you the bullying stories. "Susie Sunshine" or "Happy Harry" can be irritating during difficult circumstances.

Don't talk on and on about your (or other people's) experiences with workplace bullying. While knowing that other people have experienced the same targeting can be helpful, hearing about it for longer than 30 seconds can be annoying. It's better to be a good listener than a good talker.

Some of the saddest stories I heard were from people whose spouse or significant other was not supportive or empathic. Comments such as "I told you not to take that job" aren't helpful. He or she needs for you to be their main cheerleader and number one source of support and encouragement.

Other forms of zero encouragement or lack of support include:

- Not wanting to hear the target talk about the bullying.
- Telling the target to not mention his successes and accomplishments to anyone at work and to just keep quiet.
- Pretending the bullying isn't happening at all. Just not acknowledging it.
- Changing the subject or appearing to be disinterested when the target broaches the bullying subject.
- Colleagues at work who become so afraid that they won't listen to the target discuss it or they avoid the target altogether.
- Colleagues who kiss up to the bully to attempt avoiding being the bully's next target.

Whether the target you know is a friend, relative, or colleague, they need to talk about their experience being bullied. They need for people to validate them, their experience, and their interpretation of their experience.

The "Do's"

Whether targets had good support people in their lives or wish they had, they know what was helpful to them when they were bullied and they know what else would have been helpful.

Listening with empathy is the top priority for many targets. This can include contacting the target to schedule a phone call or to meet for coffee. Once you know this person is a target for bullying, reach out to him every once in a while.

Find out how this target is coping. *Ask good questions.* Will it be possible for him to confront the bully? If so, how? In what timeframe? If not, then what is the plan? To find a new job? If so, how can you help him with new job ideas and contacts?

Remind the target that his job doesn't define him. For example, tell him, "You're defined by who you are, not by what you do."

Good supporters in the life of a bullied teacher reminded her that she was making a great impact on her students. For non-teacher targets, you can *remind them that they're making a positive impact on* _____ (fill in the blank). What belongs there? Customers? Direct reports? Improved products or services? What else?

Other supporters of targets *acknowledged the bully was jealous of the target's accomplishments* or ability to zero-in on problems that needed to be resolved. The friend or colleague then acknowledged what should have happened (such as the target being rewarded). Then adding, "It really stinks that they won't celebrate with you regarding 'ABC' accomplishment." This type of "out loud" acknowledgement helps the target to feel *validated*. "It's too bad they're so jealous of you. They should be supportive and celebrating your achievement."

Validating the target for who they are, what they've accomplished, and what they have yet to achieve is a great way to encourage the target and give her hope. When she is encouraged and hope increases, she'll be more likely to have the *ideas and energy* needed to take positive steps to change: either getting the bully to change or finding a new job.

Colleagues can help a target by *providing camaraderie* (when the bully is the type who targets several people). Even if you aren't also a target of the bully, being in the same work-place, you're probably more familiar with the bully and the company culture than any of the target's friends. Validating the target and acknowledging what is going on will be a positive move that will help the target.

When it looks like the target will need to find a new job, *making connections and introductions for him,* even just to have conversations, will be helpful. Who do you know in the same or similar industry? Who do you know in a similar field?

When you contact these people, ask them, "I wonder if you will do me a favor. My friend/colleague, John Doe, is looking to meet people in _____ (company/indus-try/etc.). Would you be willing to have a brief call with him? Can I make an introduction?"

Most people will say yes. The idea is *not* to ask if they have a job opening. That question shuts down the conversation. Your target/friend who has decided to find a new job needs to meet as many people as possible to start a conversation. The conversation opens the door. Maybe a job will open up four months from now! A conversation next week puts your target/friend on your contact's radar.

Be a connector. Be a catalyst. Ask your contacts to meet your target/friend. *Don't* tell the contact that your target/friend is the target of a bully!

These introductions you make that turn into conversations eventually turn into interviews, and those turn into a new job. You can be that great friend who made it happen!

———————

If you're in the workplace (either at the same company as your friend who is a target or at a different company), choose to be a person in that workplace who calls out bullying behaviors in others (even if those poor behaviors are subtle) when you see it or hear about it. Don't just stand by. Take action!

7

You're Not Powerless Against Workplace Bullies

"Work shouldn't hurt."

—Ruth Namie, Workplace Bullying Institute

When I first started studying and writing about subtle workplace bullying, my writing was based on my experience with one bully. As I studied more and decided to write this book, I realized I've been the target of subtle bullies several times.

As a friend of mine once asked me, "How do these people find you?" Indeed.

Being bullied seemed to happen much too often. I'll admit I occasionally asked, "Why me?"

Writing this book as a way to help other people answers the "Why me?" question. If you are—or have been—the target of a workplace bully and this book helps you put an end to it, then my experiences being bullied have not been for naught.

While I was writing a later draft of this book, I worked at a place where six bullies came to the surface. Five of those were the subtle form of bullies. One was a full-on, abusive bully. That person quit to go to another company. One subtle bully was fired. Of the remaining four subtle bullies, two of them directly targeted me. They literally played out scenarios I had already written about. It was jaw-droppingly good (for me as a writer, anyway).

But it was also stressful to me as an employee. I experienced several of the symptoms of being bullied. It was definitely affecting my health. (When the main bully was fired, I had no more chest pain and my hair stopped falling out.)

For those of you going through it right now, I feel your pain. I have felt your pain in previous workplace experiences, too.

You either need to find a way to get the bully to stop bullying you or you need to find a new job. In the meantime, you need to learn and put into practice coping strategies so that this negative experience doesn't continue to be detrimental to your health, your relationships, and your work.

The advice in this book is designed to give you ideas about how to make changes to your life to stop bullying behaviors from negatively affecting you. I hope you've started a plan and applying it to your daily life.

During the course of your career you will certainly hear about a bully at work who is bullying someone else, but not you. Don't be an enabler—confront the behavior so that it will stop. If you don't confront it, it will continue. Help out other targets by being an Advocate.

Help other targets decide if they are going to confront the bully or find a new job. If they decide to find a new job, help them do that by providing ideas and making introductions to your contacts.

- Bullies aren't just people who yell and throw things. They have many subtle methods of bullying their targets.
- Workplace bullies are hazardous to your health.
- Pay attention to your own stress signals.

- Subtle bullies look for ways to break you down.
- A subtle bully's target can be just about anyone who tolerates them.
- Use what you learned in this book to decide if you will:

    1. Choose to cope with the bully, or
    2. Confront the workplace bully in order to get him to change, or
    3. Look for a new job (and cope in the meantime)

...and then use what you learned to reach your goal.

Life is too short to tolerate mistreatment and it shouldn't be painful to go to work. Make sure as you focus on becoming free of your workplace bully and the symptoms of being bullied that you achieve the four outcomes of coaching:

Awareness: This is awareness of both yourself and of the environment and people around you. Awareness gives you the ability to correctly assess and interpret what is going on inside of you and around you.

Purpose: By having a solid sense of purpose you will know deep inside that what you are doing in your work has meaning and that you're a valued contributor.

Competence: Knowing you are highly competent in your work is an important outcome of coaching—to be able to perform your job well and to know that you are competent in your field.

Well-being: An overall sense of well-being in your work is the fourth outcome of good coaching. Your work and profession should provide you with a sense of well-being every day.

All of the coaching outcomes are essential for having a positive workplace experience. Don't let a bully stop you from enjoying your work. Don't let a bully endanger your health. Take back your work, your health, and your life.

Afterword

Because I've been through subtle workplace bullying a number of times, and one of my coping mechanisms is to find ways to laugh about it, I decided these workplace bullies need to get together to reform themselves.

What if a bunch of workplace bullies finally realized how bad they were and that they needed help?

Imagine a group of workplace bullies meeting in a 12-Step program in order to stop their bullying behavior. I think their 12 Steps would go like this:

The 12-Step Recovery Program for Workplace Bullies

1. I admitted that I would not want to work for myself (and neither would anyone else who was sane or not psychotic themselves).
2. I determined that the only person who could help me fix my ways was Dr. Phil, Tom Peters, or God; and God was the only one willing to work for free.
3. I delegated my bullying ways to God, as no one else could possibly understand me.
4. I made a searching and fearless moral inventory of myself and found there was extensive shrinkage.
5. I admitted to God, to myself, and to the guy at the toll booth the exact nature of my bullying managerial ways.
6. I stood in a thunderstorm with foil on my head waiting for God to remove my bullying and jerky ways, but all that got removed was my neighbor's elm tree when lightening hit next door.
7. I sent God an email asking him to remove my bullying character, and I still have not seen the "read receipt" I requested.

8. I stood in front of my office building with a lunch board asking for forgiveness from my fellow workers.
9. I tried calling my ex-employees but they must have Caller ID, as no one picked up.
10. I continue to take periodic personal inventories, and the good news is that the shrinkage is down (but spoilage is way up).
11. I sought, through prayer and meditation, to improve my conscious contact with God. I'm still waiting for God to respond to my email, but I guess he has a bigger backlog than I do.
12. Having had a spiritual awakening as the result of these steps, I tried to start a *workplace bullies support group*, but everyone stopped coming after the first meeting.

Appendix

In chapter 3, "Workplace Bullies are Bad for Business," you read about the cost to a company of keeping a bully on staff. On the flipside of that topic are companies where employees are happy. They rate their companies highly on surveys that seek to find out which companies employees most enjoy working for and why.

There is very little bullying going on at the highly rated companies. Those corporations also offer their employees other positive incentives which increase employee happiness.

I didn't want to end this book without giving you more information about this issue. If you arm yourself with this information, in addition to the data about the bully's cost to the company, you'll have that much more to tell management (if they will listen) about why they should strive to eradicate bullying from your workplace.

Do Companies Perform Better When Employees are Happy?

Being the target of a *bully-lite* made me into a very unhappy employee. Would you say the same is true for you? If bullying is allowed to go on at a company unchecked, it's likely there are many people at that company who are unhappy.

Guess what? When employees at a company are unhappy with circumstances at work, it affects their performance and trickles down to the income statement of the company in terms of lower revenue and higher expenses; in a word, lower net profit.

Are you familiar with those lists of companies that come out every year, including the one about "best companies to work for"? It turns out, not only employees like working at those companies. Smart investors like those companies, too!

After following the companies that make it on the "best to work for" lists, studies show that, as a group, they have higher returns than the S&P 500. Jerome Dodson, president of Parnassus Funds, began the *Parnassus Endeavor Fund* that invests exclusively in US-based companies with a track record from being highly rated by employees as a place where they enjoy their work and the work environment.

Besides good pay and great benefits, employees rating these companies also liked going to work every day and enjoyed working with their colleagues. (Think about it: Haven't you worked at places where the pay and benefits were excellent but you had a bully who turned what would have been a great career experience into a miserable experience?)

In the first eight years of running this particular Parnassus fund, its annualized return was 9.63%. (The S&P 500 at the same time was 5.58%.) Even during a recession the fund out-performed the S&P.

I think this says a lot about the cost of having unhappy, stressed-out employees. *Companies are missing out on greater profits by keeping workplace bullies employed.*

I believe companies that work to eliminate workplace bullying in all its forms (subtle and not-so-subtle) leads to a happier workforce which leads to higher profits!

While I was working on this book, a representative from a textbook company in South Africa contacted me about an article I wrote about corporate leadership, requesting to include the article in their textbook for organizational development. Leaders at businesses across the world can heed the advice in the article in order to create a productive work environment that leads to a more profitable business.

In order to continue promoting a healthy, happy, productive work environment that leads to higher profit, I'll reprint the article here:

Create a Positive, Productive Work Environment at Your Company and Reap the Benefits

Have you ever experienced a work environment that's very positive? You look forward to being there, in that place, with those people, working on those projects. It's energizing—not in a "cheerleader/rah-rah" manner—but, overall, it just gives you a positive feeling of energy. I've worked in some positive work environments like that and it's made a huge difference in the outcome of the department or company.

It's commonly known that when we feel good, we are more energized, we work better, and we're more creative and productive. If you picture our brains like motors, *then feeling good* is like lubrication to the brain. Mental efficiency increases, memory becomes more acute, our understanding increases, and we make better decisions.

A key leadership quality is the ability to inspire positive feelings in others, which leads to the outcomes listed above. When you're a leader, how can you generate this for other people?

Your challenge is to find a balance between developing a positive work environment and helping employees to create good working relationships with others, and focusing on your area's (or company's) performance goals.

A study of 62 companies, their CEOs, and their top management teams assessed their enthusiasm, energy, and determination. It also reviewed the amount of conflict the top teams experienced in personality clashes, friction in meetings, and emotional conflicts (i.e. not disagreements about ideas). The study concluded that the more positive the overall moods were of people in the top management levels, the more cooperatively they worked together and the better the company's results at the bottom line. In contrast, the longer a company was run by a management team that did not get along, the poorer the company's result.

Common sense tells us that if employees' moods are up, they will more likely do what it takes to please customers, thereby increasing sales. Leaders can play a role in this. Since emotions are contagious, leaders have a bigger responsibility for creating and sustaining the moods of their employees. By managing their own moods, leaders can drive the customer service climate at their company and influence employees to do more for customers.

Some research has shown that for every 1% improvement in service climate, there is a 2% increase in revenue. In *Primal Leadership* (2002), Goleman, Boyatzis, and McKee reported that "how people feel about working at a company can account for 20 to 30% of business performance."

Executive coaching can help leaders create and maintain positive environments and emotions in the midst of challenges. Becoming aware of your own tendencies and learning how to improve them goes a long way toward creating a positive, energizing work environment.

While the environment of the workplace is not the only thing that determines a business' performance, it can be a sizable piece of it. Research by the Gallup organization and the Hay Group found that 50 to 70% of how employees perceive their company's environment reflects the choices of the leaders. They found that the bosses create the conditions that directly affect people's moods at work and their ability to work well together and with customers.

So what can leaders do to elicit sincere positive emotions from employees?

First, they must become aware of their own emotional tendencies and how their emotions affect others in the workplace.

Second, they can develop a plan to make changes to their own communication style to emit emotions that create an environment that is positively contagious to those around them. This plan needs to be strategic in its intention and attention, without being manipulative of others.

Leaders who have managers reporting to them will eventually want to include those managers in developing the same type of plan for themselves.

Third, after several months of making and sustaining changes to their own emotional aura, leaders should expect to enjoy the fruit of their change in the form of happier, more enthusiastic employees who consider their work environments in a very positive light, and who are (mostly consistently) more focused, productive, and cooperative.

A harmonious, energizing work environment is where I want to be. How about you?

What can you start to do this week to begin creating a more positive workplace?

EzineArticles.com, November 23, 2005
http://bit.ly/1qN6lqz

You Can Both Treat Employees Well *and* Make a Profit

One way that corporate executives keep bullies on the payroll is by having the opinion that either we can treat employees well and have a great company where everyone likes to come to work, *or* we can have a company that makes a profit. This is a sad way in which to think about business.

If you believe this is the thinking of the leadership at your company (or even if you're not sure), you might be able to help people at the company understand that it is possible for a business to be highly rated by its employees *and* for that business to make a profit annually.

Years ago a good friend discussed with me the difference between "either/or" and "both/and" thinking.

In the western part of the world, we usually think in terms of "either/or," such as "It's either 'A' or 'B.'" In the eastern part of the world, however, people tend to think in terms of "both/and," such as "It's 'A' and 'B'," or "We can get results 'A' and 'B.'"

As I was writing this book, Kip Tindell, the CEO of Container Store, wrote in a company prospectus that a company exists primarily to make money *or* it exists primarily to make employees happy. He also wrote he thought Milton Friedman, the late economist, believed a business exists primarily to make money.

Either/Or.

That is Kip Tindell's thinking, according to what he wrote in the prospectus. Consider what he's saying: Either a company exists to make money *or* it exists to make employees happy. Not both. And Kip believes Milton Friedman taught that a company exists to make money, not to make employees happy. Certainly not both.

Thomas Coleman, adjunct professor of Finance at the University of Chicago, Booth School of Business, disagrees with Tindell. He believes Tindell missed Milton Friedman's point. In a rebuttal, Mr. Coleman said Milton Friedman knew that treating employees well leads to having a successful business.

I can tell you it's not an "either/or" situation where a business can either exist primarily to make money *or* it can primarily exist to make employees happy.

It is wrong to think that either a company will be profitable while employees are mistreated or the employees will be treated well and the company won't be profitable. That's "either/or" thinking.

"Both/and" thinking on this subject says that treating employees well leads to having a profitable, successful business. You can treat employees well *and* have a profitable business.

When bullying exists at a workplace, it will lead to unhappy employees. Certainly the targets of a workplace bully will be unhappy. But the witnesses of such bullying will be unhappy, too. In addition, people who witness or hear about the bullying may wonder who will be the next target and wonder why the company doesn't put a stop to it. These types of thoughts do not lead to happiness at work.

If a company focuses on eradicating bullying and even preventing it in the first place, providing training for managers on leadership and finding ways to encourage employees to treat each other well, this will lead to a happier work environment. Happier employees leads to higher profit.

Therefore, you can eliminate workplace bullying *and* have a profitable business. You can create an atmosphere where employees aren't bullied *and* have a profitable business.

"Both/And"!

Credit Acceptance Corporation is one company that aimed to be rated highly by the Great Place to Work Institute. Their goal was twofold: to be named to the "FORTUNE 100 Best Companies to Work For®" and to reach financial goals that included aggressive increases in sales, net profit, and earnings per share. This was a long term plan set in 2001 which was reached in 2014.

Besides making their financial goals in 2012, Credit Acceptance's employees rated the company on surveys for improvements in communications (including two-way communication between leadership and rank-and-file employees), employee involvement in continuous improvement, quarterly surveys where leaders took appropriate action on issues employees raised, new leadership conduct rules that "guide leadership behavior across the organization" ensuring consistency in all departments, and ongoing initiatives regarding employee development. From 2001 to 2012, sales increased 154%, net profit increased 300%, and earnings per share increased 388%. The initiative to reach these goals through employee satisfaction was started by their CEO, Brett Roberts.[12]

I think the findings of the Parnassus Funds that you read about earlier is a great way to start a conversation at a company regarding how these companies that are highly rated by their employees also consistently have stock prices with annualized returns that are higher than the S&P returns. There will probably be more news about these types of findings after this book is published. Do Internet searches occasionally on "companies that are best to work for," "Parnassus

Endeavor Fund," GreatPlaceToWork.com, and any other articles you can find on the subject to stay current on the topic.

If companies that are highly rated by employees continue
to perform well and profitably, you should have good topics
to discuss with upper management and good articles to share
with them for years to come. You can be the change agent at
your company to start a trend to make it a place where people
want to be hired and join their team.

Examples of Companies that Treat Employees Well *and* Enjoy a Profit

In order to gather a list of companies where it is reported
that employees are treated well and the company is profitable
based on surveys and interviews with employees, I've listed
below companies that are, as of this writing, part of the
Parnassus Endeavor Fund and companies that are listed with
GreatPlaceToWork.com. The list on the next page is a combined
list shown alphabetically.

In an interview with a representative of Great Place to
Work Institute, I learned that their research about companies
is done with employees who rate their employers on 58 core
statements, mainly revolving around trust. The trust-related
characteristics a company is rated on are credibility, respect,
and fairness. Companies are also rated on pride and camaraderie.

Please go back to both lists online occasionally to
view their updated lists. (Do an Internet search for "Parnassus
Endeavor Fund" and GreatPlaceToWork.com.) In fact,
GreatPlaceToWork.com lists, for each company, the types of
things employees noted that they especially liked about
working for the company. Study these companies further:
What is going on at the leadership level that filters down to
the rank-and-file employees that makes the company rate
highly with employees, leading to greater profit?

- Allergan, Inc.
- Applied Materials
- Autodesk, Inc.
- The Boston Consulting Group
- Camden Property Trust
- Burns & McDonnell
- Capital One Finance Corp.
- C.H. Robinson, Inc.
- CHG Healthcare Services
- Corning, Inc.
- Credit Acceptance Corporation
- DPR Construction
- Edward Jones
- Expeditors International, Inc.
- FedEx Corp.
- Genetech
- Google, Inc.
- Hilcorp
- IBM Corp.
- Intel Corp.
- Intuit
- Mondelez International, Inc.
- QualComm, Inc.
- Quicken Loans
- Riverbed Technology
- Robert W. Baird, & Co.
- SalesForce.com
- SAS, Inc.
- Shaw Communications
- USAA

Bibliography

[1]All of the author's articles appear online. Some are on the author's website at BorgesonConsulting.com on the Articles page. Others appear on EzineArticles.com.

[2]Workplace Bullying Institute, 2012 Instant Poll D, Impact of Workplace Bullying on Individuals' Health. Gary Namie, PhD.

[3]Workplace Bullying Institute, 2013 Instant Poll H, First Time Abusers in Bullied Targets' Lives. Gary Namie, PhD.

[4]Workplace Bullying Institute, 2012 Instant Poll D, Impact of Workplace Bullying on Individuals' Health. Gary Namie, PhD.

[5]John Gottman, PhD, *Why Marriages Succeed or Fail* (Simon & Schuster Paperbacks, 1994.), pgs 68+.

[6]Robert I. Sutton, PhD, *The No Asshole Rule* (Warner Business Books, 2007), pgs 45+.

[7]Workplace Bullying Institute, 2014 WBI US Workplace Bullying Survey, February 2014.

[8]"Stress Relief from Laughter? It's No Joke," by Mayo Clinic Staff. MayoClinic.org

[9]M. J. Ryan's blog on MJ-Ryan.com

[10]Workplace Bullying Institute, 2013 Instant Poll D, The Timing and Results of Targets Confronting Bullies at Work. Gary Namie, PhD.

[11]"Ameet Sachdav, "Container Store CEO disses late economist Milton Friedman," *Chicago Tribune,* October 4, 2013.

[12]Jessica Rohman "Culture Without Compromise: One Company's Journey in Building a Great Place to Work as a Strategic Business Imperative: Credit Acceptance Case Study," www.greatplacetowork.com

Chapter Quotations

Ch. 1 – Jay Carter, Psy.D, *Nasty People* (McGraw Hill, 2003), pg 93.

Ch. 2 – Robert I. Sutton, PhD, *The No Asshole Rule* (Warner Business Books, 2007), pg 9.

Ch. 3 – Jerome Dodson, President, Parnassus Investments, as quoted in an online article by Mark Crowley in "The Proof is in the Profits: America's Happiest Companies Make More Money," *Fast Company*, February 22, 2013.

Ch. 4 – Psalm 73: 8-10. Scripture taken from *The Message*. Copyright © 1993, 1994, 1995, 1996, 2000, 2001, 2002. Used by permission of NavPress Publishing Group.

Ch. 5 – Andrew A. Rooney, *And More by Andy Rooney* Warner Books Edition, Copyright © 1979, 1980, 1981, 1982 by Essay Productions, Inc. All rights reserved.

Ch. 6 – Desmond Tutu, electronically retrieved at http://www.goodreads.com/quotes/tag/bullying

Ch. 7 – Ruth Namie, Workplace Bullying Institute, electronically retrieved at http://www.workplacebullying.org

Epigraph, pg. viii – Matthew 10:28. Scripture taken from *The Message*. Copyright © 1993, 1994, 1995, 1996, 2000, 2001, 2002. Used by permission of NavPress Publishing Group.

About the Author

Glory Borgeson is a consultant and business coach with over 25 years' experience in the areas of finance, technology, system implementations, change management, small business, and leadership development. Through her experiences as a corporate employee, and even later as a consultant, she learned about the subtle forms of workplace bullying.

Having never experienced being bullied in school or in the workplace while still a student, she was surprised at some of the bad behavior she encountered early in her career. However, she didn't label it as bullying at that time.

Writing about workplace bullying, and finally defining it as subtle workplace bullying, came later in Glory's career while working as a consultant. At that time, when an individual at a client company targeted her with subtle bullying behaviors, it was so isolated that, as a non-employee of the company, Glory easily separated herself from it emotionally and began writing about the experience.

Over the next several years of research into the phenomenon of subtle workplace bullying, it dawned on Glory one day, "I've been through this before." Memories flooded her mind from her earliest post-college jobs of subtle bad behaviors coming from a few bosses and colleagues. Memories of symptoms such as headaches, sleeplessness, anxiety, loss of concentration, and others came to mind as well.

While interviewing bullied targets for the book, similar stories created a larger picture of the subtle workplace bully. Glory heard stories from targets about enduring the subtle bullying for years (and the accompanying symptoms), confronting the bully only to later have that backfire, quitting the job without another job in place (or taking a low level job to get away from the bully quickly), or taking some other type of risk that the target normally wouldn't have taken if they had not been bullied. Glory had already experienced all of these things.

Glory wrote the book to offer a practical guide to targets of a subtle workplace bully to help them end the bullying in their lives.

Glory Borgeson has been a board member of several non-profit organizations. She holds a B.A. from Augustana College and is a graduate of B/Coach Systems, LLC, a business coach training company.

Glory speaks and writes about a variety of topics of interest to business owners, corporate executives, college students considering their first post-collegiate job, and subtle workplace bullying. Visit her website at www.GloryBorgeson.com for current information regarding recent articles, speaking topics, coaching programs, and more information about workplace bullying.

Glory is also the author of the following books:

Catapult Your Business to New Heights: Sure-Fire Strategies to Increase Profit

Brand Yourself! for College Students: How to Use Personal Branding to Get the Job You Want

Printed in Great Britain
by Amazon